Magic Guidebooks

Universal Studios®

Orlando Florida

2019

**FAST AND INFORMATIVE
VACATION PLANNING**

Insider Secrets, Hotel & Dining Reviews, and Tips for Universal Studios Florida, Islands of Adventure, The Wizarding World of Harry Potter, Volcano Bay, CityWalk, & More!

Magic Guidebooks
Universal Orlando 2019

• **A Fun and Fast Read** Packed with Insider Information and Tips

• **Covers the Entire Universal Orlando Resort** including Universal Studios Florida, Universal's Islands of Adventure, Universal's Volcano Bay Water Park, and Universal CityWalk

• **The Wizarding World of Harry Potter** in Detail! Learn the Best Tips for Experiencing the Magic as Well as Coverage of the New *Harry Potter* Roller Coaster Debuting in 2019!

• **Money-Saving Tips** for Tickets, Hotels, Travel, Dining, and More

• **Honest Ride and Restaurant Reviews** with Recommendations

• **Universal Dining Plan** Review, Tips, and More

• **Hotel Reviews Near Universal**, Hidden Mickeys, and Magic Details Found All Over the Resort

• **Pre-Planned Ride Lists** to Help Fit All of the Fun in Without the Need of Express Pass!

Reading Level
AGES 10 TO ADULT!

Table of Contents

GET UPDATES!

Universal Orlando is always changing—but we'll keep you updated!

Sign up for our FREE e-mail list:
www.magicguidebooks.com/signup

(We will never spam you or sell your information.)

Wishing you a magical vacation!
Magic Guidebooks

ABOUT THIS GUIDEBOOK

MAGIC GUIDEBOOKS

When developing and writing this book, we had *you* in mind. Maybe you're a first-time visitor to the Universal Orlando Resort, or perhaps you've frequented it over the years. Wherever you come from and whatever your experience, we wanted to provide a complete guide from start to finish, while giving a critique of the Universal Orlando Resort. The purpose of this guide is to provide *real* advice covering the many attractions, restaurants, and hotels from the Universal Studios and beyond.

Who are we? Well, we're theme park enthusiasts who spend a lot of time gathering first-hand knowledge and experiences from all around the world. We've written guidebooks to Disneyland and Walt Disney World, and now we're tackling the fun of the Universal Studios Orlando Resort! Advice from this guide is crafted from our trial and error—and now we're passing the fruit of our hard work on to you!

Keep in mind that this guide is an "unofficial edition," meaning that we are not affiliated with the Universal Orlando Resort, its parent company, and nor have we ever been. We are simply theme park enthusiasts who are giving an honest opinion on what the resort has to offer. Though we call ourselves "fans" and do our best to keep a fun feel, we're also critical of the resort when necessary. Overall, we want this guide to be fun, fast, and informative!

FOR UNIVERSAL NEWBIES

If you've never been to the Universal Orlando Resort before, this book is perfect for you! We've crammed our guide with tidbits about the best food, attraction recommendations, hotel pros/cons, and so much more. We'll fill you in on the Resort's lingo, history, and even its future. In the end, you'll have the knowledge of a pro!

FOR RETURN VISITORS

The Universal Orlando Resort is a constantly changing place. From exciting themed dining to upcoming thrilling attractions, *anything* could happen next! If you haven't been to Universal Orlando in ten years, this guide is a great fit.

However, if you visit every week, you probably won't learn much. That, of course, doesn't mean that you won't learn *anything*, but you're likely already a pro and a guide to a park that's essentially your second home won't be much use. Still, if you're curious, we welcome you along for the ride! Even as often as we go, we still learned *a lot* from researching for this book. Also, if you've read our Walt Disney World guide, this book may sound a bit repetitive. A lot of information in this guide is available (almost word-for-word) in our WDW version. However, this guide goes into much more detail!

A WORD FOR ALL

Since Universal Orlando updates so frequently, some of the items in this guide will change even weeks after its publication. Restaurants in CityWalk might close, attractions may be re-themed, popular food items could become discontinued... To patch this, we send updates via our free e-mail newsletter to our readers. If you'd like to be updated, visit our website and sign up today: **www.magicguidebooks.com/list** (don't worry, we won't spam you). On our website, we also keep a list of ride and attraction refurbishments, so you'll learn which experiences might be unavailable during your vacation—check it out!

CHAPTER ONE

INTRODUCTION TO UNIVERSAL ORLANDO

A BRIEF HISTORY

In 1986, after the success of Universal Studios Hollywood and Walt Disney World, Universal broke ground on a new world-class theme park. Utilizing Florida's warm, tropical weather and abundance of land, the movie studio—along with co-founder, Steven Spielberg—began designing attractions for a new set of tourists. While its Hollywood sister park invited guests inside actual film studios, Universal Studios Florida would focus on "riding the movies."

Universal's new, exciting theme park brought guests into the treacherous waters of the movie *Jaws*, the past with *Back to the Future*: The Ride, and even to E.T.'s home planet. Keeping with its slogan of "Ride the Movies" Universal Orlando bases many of its attractions on 3-D motion simulators and live entertainment shows based on popular films. Currently, Transformers: The Ride, *Despicable Me*: Minion Mayhem, and The Simpsons: The Ride, all use motion simulation with enormous screens and automated moving seats to propel guests into storylines. However, Universal also has classic rollercoasters with Hollywood Rip Ride Rockit and Revenge of the Mummy.

With over 10 million visitors in 2017, Universal Studios Florida is one of the most visited theme parks in the world w. Its scene of a Hollywood backlot and attractions based on unforgettable movies has proven popular over the years. With more rides and space than its Hollywood predecessor, Florida's version is a thrilling and unforgettable time for movie and thrill ride lovers.

ISLANDS OF ADVENTURE HISTORY

Universal Studios Florida continued its legacy of world-class entertainment when it broke ground in May 1999 with Islands of Adventure. This theme park is comprised of eight "islands" placed across a massive lagoon. Every island is captivating and themed from popular franchises like *Harry Potter*, *Jurassic Park*, Marvel Comics, and Dr. Seuss. While Universal Studios Florida immerses guests in a Hollywood backlot, Islands of Adventure brings fictional worlds to life. Jurassic Park Island is filled with palm trees and dinos while Hogsmeade Village plunges guests into the magical, snow-covered world of *Harry Potter*.

Islands of Adventure feels more like a long-lost Disney theme park with its perfect attention to detail. Waterfalls, foliage, and well-crafted rides bring both smiles and thrills to its visitors. Young kids will love the colorful and slow-paced world of Seuss Landing while thrill-riders will seek out Marvel Island's looping Hulk coaster.

Don't worry *Harry Potter* fans, we haven't left you out! Hogsmeade Village is the magical destination you've been searching for your entire life. With sweet Butterbeer carts, working wands, magical gift shops, and even a chance to enter Hogwarts Castle, you might spend half of your day in Hogsmeade, never wishing to return home!

If you haven't figured it out by now, we absolutely love Universal's Islands of Adventure. While it pulls in about a million fewer visitors than Universal Studios, it's by far the better park. Even though we love Universal Studios, too, Islands brings theme park immersion to a new level that the Studios does not. Be sure to add Islands of Adventure to your must-see theme park list!

WHICH PARK SHOULD I VISIT?

If you can't decide which park to visit, we *highly* recommend both! If you purchase a park-to-park ticket, you can take the bonus ride, the Hogwarts Express, which connects the two theme parks by a gentle and fun train ride. Both parks have *Harry Potter*-themed attractions, with Hogsmeade Village in Islands of Adventure and Diagon Alley in Universal Studios Florida.

Though Hogsmeade is stunning and home to a few more attractions, Diagon Alley is somehow even more breathtaking. You'll magically enter the area (we won't tell you how—it's a surprise for when you get there) and visit shops, dark back alleys, and even the goblin-run Gringotts bank! The centerpiece of Diagon Alley is a life-size fire-breathing dragon. Yes, *real* fire!

If you haven't already realized, there's a lot to cover before your visit. From *Harry Potter* to Universal CityWalk to Volcano Bay (which we haven't even mentioned yet), this guide covers insider tips and reviews for one of the greatest theme park resorts in the world: Universal Studios Orlando!

WHAT TO EXPECT DURING YOUR VACATION

Orlando, Florida is an ideal location for a theme park because of its year-long sunshine. Likely, as you arrive, you'll see the sun shining with white tufts of cottony clouds. Many times, especially in the late afternoon, it'll be cloudy and gray for an hour or so. Thunderstorms, especially in the summer months, will sweep by and leave as quickly as they came. It's common for it to rain each day in this part of Florida, but fortunately, it doesn't last for long. For most of the year, the humidity is high in central Florida— sometimes even 100% saturating the air. It can feel a bit stifling, but the resorts and parks prepare for this. Air conditioning pumps in every car, hotel, and indoor ride to help you enjoy your stay.

The parks are large and filled with people happy to enjoy the magic of the movies that Universal brings to life. You'll see visitors from all over the world experiencing attractions with you. Since the Universal theme parks promise more thrills than the Walt Disney World parks, tweens and teens especially love it here.

THE WIZARDING WORLD OF HARRY POTTER

You've never stepped inside of a place like The Wizarding World of Harry Potter. The magic of J. K. Rowling's best-selling book series and record-breaking films, transports guests into a real-life wizarding world where it feels like anything can happen! Watch visitors stroll the streets in Hogwarts robes (yes, it's socially acceptable for anyone of any age to dress as a wizard here) and wave their wands to "magically" activate key spots in both parks.

Universal pulls its guests into the magic of the movies while delivering a top-notch experience for all. The details in the lands of Hogsmeade Village (Islands of Adventure) and Diagon Alley (Universal Studios Florida) are ingenious and are instantly captivating. Plus, the delicious treats like a non-alcoholic Butterbeer drink and assortments of magical snacks will have your tastebuds popping (don't worry adults 21 and older, they have *Harry Potter*-inspired alcoholic beverages, too)! Not only will your photos of The Wizarding World seem unreal, but so will your memories.

PHRASES AROUND UNIVERSAL

The Universal Studios Orlando Resort – The area that encompasses all of its theme parks (Universal Studios Florida, Islands of Adventure, and Volcano Bay), the resort hotels, and the CityWalk entertainment area.

Park-to-Park Ticket – A ticket that allows you to visit two or three of the Universal Studios Orlando parks, as many times as you'd like during that day. To ride the Hogwarts Express train, you will need a Park-to-Park ticket.

Universal Express Pass and Express Pass Unlimited – For an additional cost, you can buy your way to the front of the lines. Express Pass allows one skip per ride in a day, while Express Pass Unlimited allows you to skip as many times as you'd like. If you are staying at a premium Universal Orlando Resort hotel, like The Hard Rock, you will get Express Pass Unlimited included complimentary during your stay (more on this later).

Single Rider Line – A fast way to get on the rides as long as you don't mind riding without the rest of your party. Not every ride has this feature, but the popular ones often do.

Universal Orlando App – An Apple and Android application that allows you to check wait times, sync a credit card to your ticket or hotel key, and more.

Early Park Admission – If you're staying on property, you can get into the parks an hour early on select days.

Dark Ride – An indoor ride set in a dark building.

Universal Dining Plan – Pre-purchased meal plans to select eateries around the Universal Orlando Resort.

3D – The use of 3D glasses during the ride or attraction.

4D – The use of 3D glasses with added effects like splashing water and rumbling seats.

TapuTapu – A waterproof bracelet used at the Volcano Bay Water Park in order to reserve ride times and more. This device comes with your Volcano Bay admission and you need to return it before leaving the water park (more on this later).

Animatronic – Robotic characters typically used in stage shows and rides.

Halloween Horror Nights (HHN) – A scary, horror-filled takeover of Universal Studios. Walk through mazes filled with actors playing murderers and monsters. This popular event is secondary ticket price and shows from mid-September to early November.

PHRASES AND WORDS FOR THIS GUIDEBOOK

⋆ **Magic Tips** ⋆ – These are special insider tips and secrets! Magic Tips are designed to:
- Save time waiting in lines
- Get the best viewing areas for shows and parades
- Save money booking
- Plus, many more useful hacks!

RIDE LEVELS

Everyone – Perfect for all ages
Family – Suited for all ages, but geared toward families with kids
Young Kids – Children 2-5
Kids – Children ages 6-9
Tweens – Children ages 10-12
Teens – Young people ages 13-17
Adults – People ages 18+
Thrill Riders – Those looking for the maximum thrill. Whether it's a ride with loops like the Hulk Coaster or the high-dropping Doctor Doom's Fearfall, this attraction level is not for the faint of heart.

CONTACT INFORMATION

General – Visit for booking and reservations:
www.UniversalOrlando.com

Customer Service – For booking and general questions
1 (407) 363-8000

Orbitz.com/deals – For special promotions (look for codes up to 15% Off hotels).

Bookit.com/coupon-codes – Search here for discounts on flights, hotels, and ticket bundles.

Amextravel.com – If you have an American Express Card, this can save you, plus earn more rewards.

Our Website – For updates on the Universal Orlando Resort and discounts, visit: www.magicguidebooks.com

CHAPTER TWO

PLANNING YOUR VACATION

PLANNING WHEN TO VISIT

Whether you are choosing dates or already have your vacation slot picked, we cover the day-by-day and month-by-month calendar for Universal. All parks tend to experience the same influxes of crowd size, so we'll keep it simple and group the entire resort together. It's important to know the crowd size so that you can plan accordingly to experience the attractions you desire. Rest assured, we have tips for staying ahead of the crowds even on the busiest days!

In this chapter, we will walk you through the choices of travel and our recommendations for saving time and money. Choosing a time for your vacation may not be entirely up to you. It could depend on your work schedule, your travel schedule, or your children's vacation days from school. Whether you have flexible travel days or not, we have laid out a month-by-month breakdown of what to expect when you visit Orlando. We also give you tips on how to avoid the long lines and more to save you time and make your stay a magical one!

MOST RECOMMENDED MONTHS

1. **September**

Summer weather continues throughout September in Central

Florida. Expect far fewer crowds than in June, July, and August. Halloween decorations will spread throughout the Universal Studios Florida most of the month. The popular Halloween Horror Nights also begins in the middle of September. While the weekends for this event will be packed, the weekdays have the thinnest crowds.

2. **February**
The resort typically has fewer crowds at this time, though weekends can be fairly busy. Still, we find that February is one of the better months for cooler weather, sparse crowds, and less expensive hotel rates.

3. **October**
Universal Orlando continues to come alive during Halloween with typically perfect weather. Scary decorations and creatures await you! Like in September, weekends become crowded, but the weekdays see much shorter wait times. However, Halloween Horror Nights tends to stay popular every night during October. Expect warm, humid weather this month.

LEAST RECOMMENDED MONTHS

1. **July**
Massive crowds from all over the world flood Orlando. Expect long lines, and the hottest, most humid weather of the year.

2. **December**
While park guests are treated to holiday decor and special attractions, the crowds are some of the most massive. If you must go in December, we recommend the first week.

3. **August**
Similar to July with the crowds, but August doesn't get as busy until after the first week. Keep in mind that the weather is blazing hot in Central Florida in August.

Note: Are you planning to be at the resort during one of our least recommended months? Don't worry! This guide will help you avoid those long lines. Be sure to follow one of our pre-planned attraction lists at the end of the book — we use them ourselves, and they can save you hours of time waiting in lines (or avoid them altogether).

DAY BREAKDOWN

Sunday
Weekend crowds, but far less than Saturday.

Monday
Often Mondays can be just as crowded as Sundays because guests take off extra days to avoid weekend traffic. Mondays directly after a holiday can also be very packed.

Tuesday
Our most recommended day for fewest crowds and the shortest lines.

Wednesday
Our second most recommended day for fewest crowds and shortest lines.

Thursday
Third most recommended day for fewest crowds, but still busier than most Tuesdays and Wednesdays.

Friday
Less busy in the morning, but busiest in the evening after school when the locals tend to visit. CityWalk can be open later but gets swamped with Floridians experiencing the nightlife.

Saturday
By far, the busiest day at the resort.

BEST DAYS TO VISIT

These days always depend on the month, but this is a general idea of how to avoid the largest crowds.

1. The 1st or 2nd weeks in February (especially Tuesdays and Wednesdays)
2. The last week in January (unless it's near the Martin Luther King, Jr. Day Holiday on the 3rd Monday of January)
3. Second week of September (but not around Labor Day)

MORE DATES TO CONSIDER

Weekdays – Like we said before, weekdays are the best times to plan your trip!

Holidays – These are the busiest times to visit because everyone has them off. Here is the list of holidays:

• Christmas (all week)
• New Year's (all week)
• Thanksgiving (all week)
• Easter (all week)
• The 4th of July (all week)
• Memorial Day weekend
• Labor Day weekend
• Martin Luther King Jr. weekend
• Presidents' Day weekend
• Columbus Day
• Veteran's Day weekend
• Mother's Day
• Father's Day (even more crowed than Mother's Day)

MORE TIPS

Universal's tier pricing will be higher ("Anytime" pricing) on more crowded days and lower ("Value" pricing) on less crowded days. You can view a calendar at **www.UniversalOrlando.com** to see how busy they anticipate your visit to be. We also expect that the opening of Star Wars: Galaxy's Edge at Disney's Hollywood Studios park will influence attendance at Universal Orlando. This new, Star Wars-inspired land is expected to open late fall of 2019 at Walt Disney World, but the crowds will likely visit Universal to see Harry Potter attractions as well.

MONTH BREAKDOWN

JANUARY

Overview: January is busy in the first two weeks, and generally less busy after that. The first week will be crowded from and filled with holiday attractions and decorations lighting the resort.

Weather: Mid-70°F (mid-20°C) during the day and chilly at night (sometimes in the 40°'s F / 4-9° C). The humidity is low.

Least Crowded Days: The last week in January

Most Crowded: The first two weeks (especially around New Year's) and Martin Luther King Jr. Weekend (Friday through Monday).

New Year's EVE Celebration:
CityWalk hosts a massive annual event on December 31st called EVE. Live DJs, decorations, and food all come with the event that lasts from 8pm until 2am. This is a separate ticketed night that can be purchased on UniversalOrlando.com usually in December.

FEBRUARY

Overview: Typically, the least crowded month to visit the Universal Orlando Resort.

Weather: Mid-70°F (mid-20°C) during the day and chilly at night (low 50°'s F / 10-12°C). Also expect far less humidity than in the summer and fall. The humidity is low.

Least Crowded Days: Any week except near Presidents' Day Weekend (Friday through Monday)

Most Crowded: President's Day Weekend (Friday through Monday).

Mardi Gras: All month, Universal Studios hosts a Mardi Gras celebration with delicious New Orleans food, music events, and stilt walkers. This is a popular event that comes with your ticket.

MARCH

Overview: March's popularity has increased recently as spring breaks spread throughout the month. If you visit in March, be sure to do so during the week, Tuesday through Thursday.

Weather: mid-70°F (21°C) during the day and chilly at night. However, March has been known to have occasional heatwaves, bringing the weather above 90°F (32°C).

Least Crowded Days: the first Tuesday, Wednesday, and Thursday of March.

Most Crowded: Last two weeks of the month for Spring break.

Mardi Gras: The event continues through March at Universal Studios.

APRIL

Overview: With spring breaks continuing through April, the end of the month tends to be the least crowded. We love visiting in April because the weather feels warm, but a lot less humid than the summer and fall months.

Weather: Low-80°F (25-28°C) during the day and cooler at night (mid-60°F / 15-19°C). The humidity is medium.

Least Crowded Days: The last two weeks of the month.

Most Crowded: The weeks before and after Easter.

MAY

Overview: Spring in Orlando is beautiful, but very warm. To most, it will feel like the Floridian summer has begun. Storms tend to pick up during this time and it might rain during the day for an hour or so. However, the rain is warm and the rides are set up for the short showers, so it shouldn't put a damper on your vacation.

Weather: Mid-70°F (21°C) during the day and sometimes chilly at night. The humidity is medium/high.

Least Crowded Days: The first two weeks of the month.

Most crowded: Memorial Day weekend (Friday through Tuesday).

Most crowded: Memorial Day weekend (Friday through Tuesday).

JUNE

Overview: Mild summer weather perfect for water rides and pool time fun!

Weather: Mid-80°F (27°C) during the day. Typically keeps warm at night. The humidity is medium/high.

Least crowded days: Tuesday, Wednesdays, and Thursdays and the first week of the month.

Most crowded: The last week of the month.

JULY

Overview: The weather heats up—often, unbearably so—and crowds from all over the world pour into the Universal Orlando Resort. Even though July is crowded, it does make a great opportunity to visit Volcano Bay and ride the many water-based attractions at the theme parks.

Weather: Low-90°F during the day, but the humidity can make July feel even warmer. The weather typically stays warm and humid at night. The humidity is high.

Least Crowded Days: Tuesday, Wednesdays, and Thursdays (unless one is July 4th)

Most Crowded: July 4th

Fourth of July:

See a fireworks spectacular at Universal Studios Florida throughout the night. This is the same fireworks display, but done with a bit more flare.

Note: As we've said before, July is the busiest month. If you are planning to visit during this time, see our tips for beating the crowds at the end of this chapter.

AUGUST

Overview: Just when you think Florida couldn't get any hotter than in July, August comes around. August is typically the hottest month. The weather continues to heat up even more and crowds continue to pour in until school begins around mid-August. However, August rarely feels as crowded as July.

Weather: Mid-90°F (32°C) during the day with usually near 100% humidity. Nights are sometimes just as warm and balmy. Showers typically occur once a day for an hour or two, but the queues for most rides have coverings. The humidity is very high.

Least Crowded Days: Tuesday, Wednesdays, and Thursdays and the last two weeks of the month.

Most Crowded: The first 2 weeks of the month.

· Magic Tips ·

Don't forget the water! Bring your own sealed bottle to save money. American Express customers as receive a free bottle of water at the American Express lounge at Universal Studios.

SEPTEMBER

Overview: More hot weather typically all month long with Halloween Horror Night beginning in the middle of them month (see October for details).

Weather: High-90°F (32°C) during the day. Typically keeps very warm at night. The humidity is very high.

Least Crowded Days: Tuesday, Wednesdays, Thursdays, and Fridays

Most Crowded: Labor Day weekend.

OCTOBER

Overview: As the weather cools, the monsters come out to play! See the scary side of Universal Orlando at the special event, Halloween Horror Nights. Decorations are also left during the daytime.

Weather: High-80°F (29-31°C) during the day, cools a bit at night. The later you go in October, the more likely tropical storms can come into play. If you are planning a visit, we recommend somewhere in the first couple of weeks. The humidity is very high.

Least Crowded Days: Tuesday, Wednesdays, and Thursdays

Most Crowded: Evenings when guests visit before Halloween Horror Nights.

SPECIAL EVENT: HALLOWEEN HORROR NIGHTS

A special event for after dark, when the parks close. See monster and horror movies and television come to life in intricate mazes, terrifying displays, and vengeful murderers running the streets. Every year the themes change, so you'll never know what to expect! Later on, we cover Halloween Horror Nights in more detail.

NOVEMBER

Overview: The holidays begin mid-November at the Universal Orlando Resort. Expect larger crowds beginning Veterans Day and onward (see December for holiday details).

Weather: High-70°F during the day, cools at night to High-50°F. The humidity is medium.

Least Crowded Days: The first week of the month.

Most Crowded: Veteran's Day weekend and Thanksgiving week.

SPECIAL EVENT: THANKSGIVING

Thursday, November 28th, 2019

If you are planning your stay during the holiday, make your reservation to one of these hotel dining experiences:

Aventura Hotel – The Urban Pantry hosts a Thanksgiving feast with traditional favorites.

Cabana Bay Beach – The Bayline Diner offers a traditional Thanksgiving lunch and dinner with turkey, mashed potatoes, stuffing, gravy, and yams for guests.

Sapphire Falls – Amatista Cookhouse offers a Thanksgiving breakfast and dinner buffet with characters (dinner only).

Royal Pacific Resort – Jake's American Bar serves breakfast and the Islands Dining Room serves a lunch and dinner character buffet with traditional Thanksgiving favorites.

Hard Rock Hotel – The Avalon Ballroom hosts a Thanksgiving Day breakfast buffet. The Kitchen Restaurant serves a Thanksgiving buffet for lunch and dinner. Expect traditional favorites as well as seafood. Characters, a magician, and other entertainment show up for this event.

Portofino Bay – Trattoria del Porto serves a lunch and dinner buffet with Thanksgiving traditional dining. Universal characters, other entertainers, and a craft table spread around the room.

DECEMBER

Overview: The holidays roll in with a *Harry Potter*-themed Christmas celebration. Not all is merry, however, as the Grinch stomps in to Seuss Landing.

Weather: Low-70°F (21-23 °C) during the day, cools at night to Low-50°F (10-12°C). The humidity is low.

Least Crowded Days: The first week of the month.

Most Crowded: The last two weeks, especially Christmas Day and New Year's Eve.

Universal Holiday Parade

The Macys Day parade floats come south to Universal Studios Florida in this exciting daytime celebration.

THE WIZARDING WORLD CHRISTMAS

Harry Potter fans, rejoice for the magic of Christmas and the Wizarding World about to spring to life. Hogsmeade and Diagon Alley are well-decorated for this stunning event. Drink hot Butterbeer while you watch the night time spectacular at Hogwarts Castle with unforgettable projections and dazzling special effects!

SPECIAL EVENT: CHRISTMAS

Wednesday, December 25th, 2019

The following hotels offer Christmas Day Feasts:

Aventura Hotel – The Urban Pantry

Cabana Bay Beach – The Bayline Diner

Sapphire Falls – Amatista Cookhouse (Christmas breakfast buffet and a Christmas dinner character buffet)

Royal Pacific Resort – Jake's American Bar serves breakfast and the Islands Dining Room serves a lunch and dinner character buffet.

Hard Rock Hotel – The Avalon Ballroom hosts a Christmas Day breakfast buffet and the Kitchen Restaurant serves a Christmas character buffet for lunch and dinner.

Portofino Bay – Trattoria del Porto serves a lunch buffet with Christmas traditional dining. Universal characters, other entertainers, and a craft table.

MORE HOLIDAY EVENTS

Hanukkah Menorah Lighting Ceremony – Hosted in each hotel at sundown during Hanukkah.

Santa Claus Visit – Santa stops by the Hard Rock Hotel, Portofino Bay, and Cabana Bay Beach Resort on select nights in December.

SPECIAL EVENT: NEW YEAR'S EVE
Wednesday, December 25th, 2019

CityWalk hosts a massive annual event on December 31st called EVE. Live DJs, special effects, and food all come with the event that lasts from 8pm until 2am.

Tickets ranges from about $110 to $200 per adult (21+ only). VIP tickets include drinks tickets and access to private bars, food, and a special entrance to avoid the crowds. Universal Annual Passholders save 10% when purchasing in advance. Prices usually increase after December 15th.

Tickets may be purchased at **UniversalOrlando.com**.

BEAT THE CROWDS

1. **Be Early** – Get to the park at open before the crowds. If you are staying at a Universal Orlando Resort hotel, you can get early entry to the *Harry Potter* attractions in both parks. Since these are the most popular areas, it can save you quite a bit of time, though the hours can start as early as 7:00am.

2. **Plan Your Day** – Follow one of our pre-set day plans at the end of this guide. We use these planners ourselves, and it will save you hours of time waiting in lines or miss them altogether!

3. **Avoid Typical Meal Times** – If you don't have a restaurant reservation, these are the times to avoid on the busy days:
    <u>Lunch:</u> Dine before 11.30am and after 2.30pm
    <u>Dinner:</u> Dine before 5.00pm and after 7.30pm

4. **Get Express Pass** – These premium passes skip the bulk of the line to most attractions at Universal Orlando. However, Express Pass does come with a steep cost (often averaging an additional $100 for both park). Express Pass Unlimited comes at no extra charge with your stay at the Hard Rock Hotel, Portofino Bay Hotel, or Royal Pacific Hotel. However, in this guide will give tips to experience the attractions without spending your money on this pass.

WHAT TO BRING

1. **What to Wear** – Shorts, t-shirts, sneakers (trainers), and tank tops are seen all around the resort for a good reason: they are comfortable. You'll be standing in the hot (and often humid) Florida sun all day, so we recommend that you dress comfortably. Even on a hot day Orlando can get chilly at night. We highly recommend taking a jacket or sweater to keep you warm during the winter.

2. **Hats and Sunglasses** – Again, the Floridian sun! It's a wonderful thing, but you don't want to get burned. Be careful of hats and sunglasses on rides (most high-speed attractions will have a compartment on the ride or a locker to store your belongings).

3. **Sunscreen** – Even on a cloudy day the ultraviolet rays from the sun can give you an uncomfortable burn. Be careful and stay protected—you don't want to ruin your vacation by looking and feeling like a boiled lobster!

4. **Stroller** – You can bring your own or rent one at one of the parks. If you're even worried a little that your child may be too tired to walk around all day, it's best to use caution and set aside extra cash for a stroller rental.

5. **Water Bottles and Snacks** – You can save money (or help any picky eaters in your party) by bringing your own snacks. Universal will allow you to bring sealed bottles of water into the parks. If you don't mind fountain water, you can refill at water fountains near any restroom for free.

6. **Hand Sanitizer** – Though we know that science tells us not to use hand sanitizer on a daily basis, it's virtually a must-have at the theme parks. Sometimes you've gone to the restroom a half hour before eating, and the lines are long to wash your hands. You'll likely touch handrails, seat cushions, and many other things that will require you to disinfect before touching food.

7. **Extra Phone Charger** – If you have a smartphone, we highly recommend an extra portable charger. We also recommend becoming familiar enough with your smartphone so that you can change on the battery-saver mode in the settings. This will prevent you from running out of juice too early while you take pictures and use the Universal Studios app.

8. **Waterproof Bag** – If you plan on riding the water attractions—like Jurassic Park River Adventure—you're likely to get wet. The last thing you want is to accidentally drench your cellphone! If your device isn't water resistant, a plastic sandwich bag for each phone to keep them dry (this also works great for wallets).

9. **A Standard Backpack** – Carry your items in one of these. Make sure it's not too large to fit on the rides. Also keep in mind that your bag will be checked by security before entering the park area. If you don't feel like lugging it around all day, rent a locker after the entrance to each park and store it in there (costs about $8 - $10 per day).

10. **Money** – The Universal Orlando Resort accepts all major credit cards and cash. However, if you are staying at a resort hotel, you can link your hotel key card to your credit card for easy paying. Volcano Bay visitors can link a credit card to their TapuTapu bracelet via the Universal Orlando application. This way you can eat and not worry about soaking your credit card or visiting a locker.

11. **Identification** – For adults, make sure you plan on bringing your government-issued ID if you plan to drink alcoholic beverages. At times, you may be asked to present ID when purchasing at shops in CityWalk.

12. **Water Resistant Clothing** – Even on the sunniest days, rainclouds can show up at the resort. Typically, the rain will last under two hours, but you don't want to wear something that can't get wet. Leave the suede shoes at home and stick to quick-drying cotton shirts. Just in case you don't want to deal with the rain, this is what we recommend bringing with you
Compact Umbrella – On rainy days, this is very handy. Don't bring a full sized umbrella, as it won't fit on rides and will be difficult to carry around.
Poncho – It might be a bit of a fashion *faux pas* to some, but a poncho could keep you and your belongings dry. Many visitors love wearing these for the water rides as well!

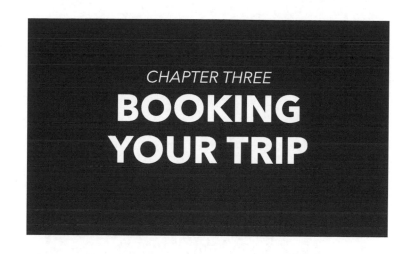

CHAPTER THREE

BOOKING YOUR TRIP

TIPS BEFORE YOUR BOOK

For all vacation planning, we always recommend booking as far in advance as possible. However, Universal often has last-minute hotel rooms that could still save you a bundle. The only exceptions are the Hard Rock and Portofino Bay hotels which tend to book up quickly. Last-minute cancellations occur and you can still get a great discount, especially during the less busy times. If you're traveling by air, we recommend Orlando International because it tends to be the least expensive and easiest to travel from. The airport is located right next to highways that will take you to Universal, which is only about 20 minutes away by car.

    If you are planning to exclusively stay at the Universal Orlando Resort, you likely won't need a rental car. Simply call a cab, ride share service, or use your hotel's transport to get from the airport to the resort. Many hotels outside of the resort will also provide free transport to the parks. Even if you are planning a day at Disney, but staying at Universal, we recommend saving money and skipping the rental car. Not only will the car cost you, but so will parking at the resort. We'll review parking cost and all transport options next.

TICKETS

Bundle

Sometimes purchasing a flight/hotel/car package from www.UniversalOrlando.com or a third party travel website can save you a lot of money. If you collect points with airlines like Southwest or Alaska, you can get even better bonuses with a bundle.

Park Ticket

Single-Day park tickets vary in pricing for each day, depending on the predicted crowd size. In other words, normal weekdays are less expensive than weekends and holidays. Universal has many options and add-on features that can be a bit difficult to understand on their website, so we've simplified it here:

Advanced Tickets Prices – Adult and Child

Save up to $20 per ticket when you purchase before the day of your visit. Child tickets are for ages 3-9. Adults are 10+. Children under 3 get in free.

Value Ticket

$115 for 1-Day, 1 Park ($110 per child) typically Mon – Thurs, not during holidays or summer.

Anytime Ticket

$124 — Use any day within a certain time period

Volcano Bay

$80 Adult and $75.00 Child per day

Park to Park

$170 Value ($165 per child) and $179 Anytime ($174 per child).Visit either park as many times as you'd like in one day.

Multi-Day Tickets

Universal will discount day tickets purchased in advance. Often, they run limited-time deals where you purchase 2 days and you get 2 days free, starting at around $200.00 for one park a day, or park to-park for around $250.00, though promotional prices vary.

Annual Passes

Universal offers several annual passes starting at $284.99 for a seasonal pass that works at both Universal Studios Florida and Universal's Islands of Adventure. Some of these annual passes have blockout dates. However, if you're visiting during a less-busy time for multiple dates, an annual pass could save you money. Annual Passes also come with several perks including free or discounted parking and event tickets, early park admission, and hotel discounts.

Parking Cost for Theme Parks

$25 for standard self-parking
$40 for "prime parking" (closest spots to the resort)
$30 for RV/Bus
Valet is also available for 2 hour windows starting at $25

· Magic Tip ·

After 6pm, self-parking is free (not valid during Halloween Horror Nights).

EXPRESS PASS

Express Pass is a paid feature that works in conjunction with your admission ticket. This unique pass allows guests to "cut the line" to nearly every attraction in Universal Studios Florida and Universal's Islands of Adventure. Express Pass allows for skipping the main line once per ride per day while Express Pass *Unlimited* allows for as many skips as they'd like. Guests can even ride an attraction over and over again, back to back!

Express Pass Unlimited starts at about $20 more than the standard Express Pass. Guests can also select Express Pass at just one park or both. The busiest days may also charge more or run out of Express Passes, so we always recommend purchasing in advance.

TIPS FOR BUYING EXPRESS PASS

1. **Get One Free** – Guests staying at the Hard Rock Hotel, Portofino Bay, or Royal Pacific Hotels get free Express Pass Unlimited as part of their room reservation. Simply use your hotel key as your Express Pass. Each member of your party will need their own room key with their name printed on it. Hotel Express Passes also work all day on your date of checkout.

2. **Book Ahead** – Universal only distributes so many Express Passes each day, so we recommend booking in advance. Express Passes are usually cheaper when booked ahead.

3. **You Can Still Buy There** – If you change your mind last minute and decide to purchase an Express Pass, see an Express Pass distributor inside of the park and upgrade your ticket (if the passes are still available). Look for the "Express Pass Sold Here" sign at vendors around the parks.

4. **Late Arrival** – On less-busy days, Universal may offer a discounted Express Pass that works after 4pm. If available, these passes can be purchased during the day at Express Pass distribution locations throughout both parks.

Notes
1. Not all Park-to-Park tickets include Volcano Bay. Only the 3-Park tickets include all three of the resort parks. You may add on Volcano Bay to your multi-day ticket at a discounted bundled price.
2. Tickets have date limitations, so be careful not to purchase too far in advance. We have seen people turned away from the gates for expired and incorrect tickets.
3. Prices may increase or decrease throughout the year.
4. Express Passes are an add-on to your Universal Studios or Island of Adventure ticket and they can be purchased together or separately, but you must have a park ticket to use Express Pass and Express Pass Unlimited.
5. Florida residents can save even more on tickets, up to $80 off ticket promotions, but you must have a valid Florida ID to get this discount. Blockout days may apply for these specially prices tickets. For more information about Florida resident discounts, visit UniversalOrlando.com.

BOOKING WITH DISCOUNTS

There are many ways to save on booking a stay at Universal Orlando. Some offers are better than others depending on the deal. Here are our most recommended booking sites based on total savings. When visiting, we often book with Orbitz for their extra discount on the hotel and then book the tickets separately through **www.UniversalOrlando.com**.

AMERICAN EXPRESS

American Express is the official credit card for the Universal Orlando Resort, which means you can use it for special perks and discounts.

1. <u>American Express Lounge</u> – Take a break in this exclusive lounge only for American Express cardholders. The lounge is located in Universal Studios Florida (not Islands of Adventure) and provides free snacks, waters, and a concierge. The lounge is located in New York City (behind the Classic Monster Cafe) and is open from 12pm – 5pm daily.

2. <u>Reserved Seating</u> — Get special reserved seating in the American Express Reserved Parade Viewing area at Universal Studios. Present your American Express Card at the viewing area across from the Brown Derby Hat Shop in Hollywood. You must get there at least 15 minutes before the parade time. Seating is first come, first served.

3. <u>Discounted Dining Plan</u> – Use your American Express card to purchase a Quick Service Universal Dining plan and receive 10% off.

Note: These offers may expire at any time.

ORBITZ.COM – *highly recommended!*
Perfect for extra hotel discounted rooms, even last minute. You still receive all of the perks including early entry and Express Pass for applicable hotels.
<u>Discount Code</u>: **www.orbitz.com/coupons**
Note: Additional discounts may not work for all Universal Orlando hotels. However, we've used them well with hotels outside of the resort.

BOOKIT.COM
- Perfect for flight/hotel packages with ticket options.
- Pros of Bookit.com:
    - Payment plans available with a down payment (no credit check required).
    - Often big discounts on flights and park tickets when you book a package.
    - Universal Orlando Resort Hotels available with all of the same benefits of booking through Universal.
    - We tend to notice that Bookit.com has a different selection of available hotel rooms than other third-party sites.
    - Bundle park tickets for discounts. Save on multiday park hopper tickets and to other parks including Universal Studios Orlando, Islands of Adventure, Volcano Bay, Walt Disney World, and more.
    - Discounted car rental options and inexpensive travel insurance available.
- Cons:
    - When you book a hotel without airfare, this website can sometimes be more expensive than other third parties.
    - Some of the better deals cannot be cancelled.
    - Often the cancellation comes with a fee. Many other companies offer free cancellation
    - Discount Code Link: **www.bookit.com/coupon-codes**

UNIVERSALORLANDO.COM – *Best for Tickets*

1. Check the website for discounts on hotels and more. Here you can book any of the resort hotels, purchase theme park tickets, and add features like Express Pass.
2. Summer Time (June – August) and Fall (September – October) typically have the lowest fares. However, Universal will offer discounts even for Spring and Winter getaways. Look for deals when booking on the website.
3. Universal Orlando also has a price-match guarantee, so if you'd rather book with them than a third party, you'll need to e-mail or fax proof of the cheaper price.

PRICELINE.COM

Great hotel selections and vacation packages on an easy-to-use site. It's hard to find promotional codes for Priceline, but they have great prices. Check Priceline's Express Deals which can save you on last-minute booking for hotel rooms in Orlando.

Military Discounts

Universal offers ticket and hotel packages for those who have served and are currently serving in the United States military. For more information and to see current deals, visit their website: **https://site.universalorlando.com/military/**

Other Sites

There are almost countless other options for finding discounts in Orlando. The best deals are typically when you bundle a flight, hotel, and park tickets as one package. Those with AAA memberships, Amex Travel offers, and other affiliations could save a bit more booking through those vendors. We recommend comparing a few third-party sites to ensure you are truly getting the best discount available for your accommodations.

CHAPTER FOUR

TRAVELING TO UNIVERSAL

INTRODUCTION

With the planning out of the way, it's time to bring
your vacation to the Universal Orlando Resort.
Getting there doesn't have to be tricky, but if you
don't plan correctly, it could feel very stressful. Most
visitors either drive or fly into Orlando International
Airport. If you have a family of three or more and
live within a comfortable driving distance, then traveling by car
might be your cheapest option. However, if you live on the West
coast or the Midwest, or internationally, is out the question.
Thankfully, there are many options to visit Universal Orlando. In
fact, you can arrive at the resort via bus, train, shuttle, or
ridesharing like Lyft!

      In this chapter, we review the several different methods of
getting to the resort. How you get there is entirely up to you, but if
you're feeling indecisive (or just need more information in order to
choose), read thoroughly to review the best choices.

BY AIRLINE

If you aren't planning a road trip and live far away from the resort,
flying will likely be your quickest method. While airlines can be
expensive at times, there are several ways to save money:

1. Compare airlines to see the best pricing.
2. Check baggage fees and allowed carry-on items. If you live on the east coast, Spirit Airlines is an *à la carte* option that can save you hundreds of dollars, especially on last-minute flights.
3. Book early, if you can, to get the best discounts.

FLIGHTS WITHIN THE U.S.A

Southwest
We love Southwest. If you grab their "Wanna Get Away" deals, you can score some great rates. Southwest works perfectly if you book ahead. However, if you are late to the game, they can get pretty pricey. We love Southwest because the staff is friendly, the aircrafts are generally comfortable for long flights, they include complimentary snacks and soft drinks, and you get 2 free checked luggage bags per person. Free bags are very hard to find these days in the United States, so this is a great deal!

Southwest doesn't charge for change fees, meaning, if you have to change your flight for whatever reason, you can do so without charge during an allotted time period (but not a refund). Because Southwest offers first-come-first-served seating, we highly recommend paying the extra money to get the "Early Bird" option. This will allow everyone in your party to pick seats together for your flight. Before boarding, you can ask their helpful staff members to assist with seating your family together, though it can't be guaranteed.

Alaska
We also love Alaska Airlines for its updated aircrafts and well-rounded service. Book early enough, and their rates are very affordable. Alaska gives you the free option to select your seat, but checked bags are often at a moderately priced additional charge. Alaska also offers free soft drinks and snacks for their flights. From the West coast, Alaska is usually one of the few airlines that offers nonstop flight. If you've never flown Alaska, we invite you to give them a try!

Delta
Delta is a premium airline that excels in what it does. While it's not as innovative with its deals as Southwest, it does deliver fantastic flights and aircrafts. This is usually our third choice above other

airlines like United or American because of Delta's quality. Those traveling from the East coast may be able to find fantastic deals when flying Delta to Orlando. However, for West coasters, Delta is often much more expensive that Southwest or Alaska.

Spirit Airlines (budget option)
This airline is an *à la carte* airline, so the first price you see is just for a seat on the plane—everything else is an extra cost. The extra costs include: picking your own seat, checking a bag or putting a bag in the overhead compartment, drinks, and snacks. If you don't mind where you sit and only need to bring a personal item, Spirit can save you some big bucks. However, once you pick a seat and opt to bring another bag (even carry-on bags are extra), the prices begin to stack. Also, Spirit Airlines doesn't have much of a customer service department in our opinion. We've had an issue with a delayed flight and no one was there to assist at the gate. However, we've had a good experience with them as well. Just understand that you usually get what you pay for and Spirit is no exception to that rule.

Frontier Airlines (budget option)
Works similarly to Spirit and can get to be very pricey. We find that Spirit tends to have more comfortable seats than Frontier. If you're only on a two-hour flight or less, you may not mind. However, Frontier is fine for last-minute flights if you're looking to save and don't need any extra pizazz. Just remember the checked bags are additional.

FROM THE UNITED KINGDOM

KLN-Royal Dutch Airlines
A standard budget airline with plenty of flights from the UK to Orlando International Airport. We've flown KLM before and found that they exceeded our expectations for the price point. You'll have a comfortable seat, efficient boarding, and quality service.

Icelandair
Another competitively priced flying option from Europe. We like Icelandair because not only do they usually have quick flights from

the UK, but they also have quality service. We avoid long layovers whenever possible, which Icelandair rarely schedules.

BY CAR

Whether you're on a road trip, staying in a neighboring city, or you live close enough to drive to the resort, driving can be a great method. On the drive you'll see the beautiful sights of Florida's wetlands before arriving at Universal Orlando.

 Car Rental: We recommend Enterprise.com or Dollar.com for car rental as they typically have great selection and the best pricing. Pre-booking before you arrive at the airport is advised.

⋆ Magic Tip ⋆
If you are just planning on staying at the Universal Orlando Resort, we don't recommend a rental car. Parking can cost $30 daily or more at the hotels and there are free transports around the resort. If, however, you plan on visiting Walt Disney World or any other parts of Florida, the car may be worth the fee.

POPULAR RENTAL CAR COMPANIES

www.Enterprise.com: You can visit the company's website or see typically better deals on Priceline.com (or bundle with your airfare and hotel booking).

www.Dollar.com: click the "specials" tab for deals.

www.Budget.com: click the "deals" tab for offers.

BY SHUTTLE OR TAXI

Hail a taxi in front of the airport and ask for a flat rate. Rates are usually around $45 each way.

MEARS

For shuttle service from the airport, we recommend Mears.
http://www.mearstransportation.com (they also have an app). Mears usually costs about $23 each way, per person. You can also pay up front for the round trip cost of $37 and they will pick you up from your hotel and return you to the airport at the end of your vacation.

Discount Code: WEB10 (to save 10%) with Mears

Note: It is customary to tip your taxi driver 15–20%, depending on your experience with the route.

BY TRAIN

Taking the train can a be relaxing and beautiful way to travel to Universal Orlando. The trains let out at the Orlando Station (or Kissimmee) and you will need to have a second transport from the train station to the resort (which is roughly 20 minutes away by car).

AMTRAK – Perfect for longer distances.
Website: www.Amtrak.com
Check the "Deals" tab for discounts.

BY BUS

There are a few great reasons to take the bus to Universal Orlando:

1. **Saves Money** – This is usually the top reason you might want to go with the bus. Airfare and the train can cost ten times the amount.
2. **It's Relaxing** – The bus can be a calming, easy way to travel from your home to the resort.
3. **A Discount** – Seniors and students can receive discounted rates on Greyhound.
4. **Greyhound** – Our top pick for bussing services. They have a great reputation and are often the fastest way with the most options to get to Orlando. Keep in mind that the Orlando Bus Station is not near Orlando International or Universal. You'll

need to take a private car into the resort or to your hotel—and that might cost you a lot of money.

BY PRIVATE CAR APP

With ride-sharing apps like Lyft taking off across the country, it may seem like a top choice for most travelers. Lyft offer private drivers in clean cars (these are not cabs).

Here are a few ways you can book:
Lyft (mobile application):
To download the application, open the App Store (Apple Devices) or GooglePlay Store (Android Devices) and search for "Lyft" in the store.
• Lyft — Their least expensive car options which seats 4, goes for around $15-$30 each way (depending on traffic)
• You can request a larger car, Lyft XL, which can seat up to 6 for an additional fee which varies by distance.
• Promo codes (typically only for first time riders):
  https://www.lyft.com/promo-coupon-code-free-rides
  (often a free or discounted first ride)
• When you are ready for your car to arrive, activate it on the app. The pickup spot is in the Express Pick-Up tunnel located on Level 2 (subject to change). The application should signal where to go. Your driver also will alert you when he/she has arrived.
• When leaving the returning to the airport, you can summon a Lyft on the app to pick up at your hotel. This is usually the same cost as traveling there.

TRANSPORT INSIDE THE UNIVERSAL ORLANDO RESORT

Water Taxis
Running every 15-30 minutes, these free taxis travel between the parks and CityWalk to Hard Rock Hotel, Loews Portofino Bay, the Royal Pacific, and Sapphire Falls. This is our favorite method to travel. The water taxis have a covering to shield from the weather and the river is fun for scenery—including the occasional turtle swimming beside the boat.

Shuttles

Free busses will shuttle you between all of the hotels to the parks and CityWalk. The shuttles run about every 15 minutes.

Walk

All resort hotels have walking paths to the parks, with Hard Rock being the closest at 5 minutes. The rest are about 10-15 minute walks on paths with signs directing you.

CHAPTER FIVE

UNIVERSAL STUDIOS FLORIDA

THEMED AREAS

The original Universal Studios Orlando theme park brings guests into a faux Hollywood studio backlot. Yet, so that the theme doesn't tire, Universal created several different areas to explore. From the streets of New York City to the magical world of *Harry Potter*, Universal Studios Florida sets out to impress with thrills.

Production Central

Right out the entrance, you'll be surrounded by large soundstages that house family-friendly attractions like *Despicable Me* Minion Mayhem and Shrek 4-D. Production Central eventually turns into a small outdoor amphitheater where live concerts are sometimes hosted.

New York

The details of the New York lot are incredible! From pizzerias to the museum facade that hosts the Revenge of the Mummy roller coaster, you'll feel part of a real-life New York movie set!

San Francisco

Like New York, but with a West coast vibe. San Francisco runs along a studio lagoon and features the high-speed simulator, Fast and the Furious: Supercharged.

Diagon Alley – The Wizarding World of Harry Potter
Right out of the *Harry Potter* films comes a stunning London scene. You'll have to find your way inside of Diagon Alley's hidden entrance, but once you do, you'll be magically transported into the Wizarding World of Harry Potter. Robed witches and wizards crowd this land filled with shops, enchanted eateries, and the Gringotts bank. Most noticeably will be the giant, fire-breathing dragon at the end of the alley!

World Expo
A swanky, World Expo-themed area with a theatre and the crazy alien shootout ride, Men in Black Alien Attack!

Springfield: Home of the Simpsons
Experience animated fun on The Simpsons Ride! Adults can grab a beer at Moe's Tavern and families can enjoy the best donut ever, The Big Pink, at Lard Lads.

Woody Woodpecker's Kidzone
Universal's perfect spot for families with young kids. Kids can see Barney the purple dinosaur, play in a Curious George play zone, and even fly to E.T.'s home planet.

Hollywood
Rounding off the backlot theme, Hollywood brings mid-century charm to its surrounding sound stages and facades. This area is a little outdated, but fun nonetheless with a nighttime show and fireworks over the lagoon.

PRODUCTION CENTRAL

RIDES

DESPICABLE ME MINION MAYHEM

Description: A 3D motion simulation ride with moving seats that follows characters from the *Despicable Me* animated film series.

Type: Motion Simulation Ride

Perfect for: Kids, Tweens, Family

Height Restriction: 40"

Review: Even if you're not a fan of *Despicable Me*, this zany and hilarious motion simulation ride should be on your list. The ride line gets pretty long throughout the day, so we recommend experiencing this attraction at the early on to avoid the increasing wait times.

Note: *Non-moving seats are available.*

SHREK 4-D

Description: A 4D theater show starring the characters from the Shrek franchise.

Type: 3D Theater Show with added special effects

Perfect for: Kids, Tweens, Family

Height Restriction: None

Review: Children 12 and under will likely enjoy Shrek 4-D the most. Hilarious characters and 3D effects, gives this attraction lots entertainment value. However, Adults and Teens may find Shrek a little too silly, though the 4D effects like water spritzes and moving seats keep everyone on their toes.

Note: *Non-moving seats are available.*

HOLLYWOOD RIP RIDE ROCKIT

Description: A high-speed steel roller coaster where you pick the soundtrack.

Perfect for: Thrill Riders

Height Restriction: 51" minimum and 79" maximum
Car: 2 riders per row
Single Rider Available
Review: The Rip Ride Rockit has a very cool feature of selecting your own music for the ride. Pick from around 30 different songs from pop and rock to country and dance before you ride. Then you'll soar over 16 stories in the sky before dropping nearly straight down at up to 65 miles per hour. An exciting, high-speed coaster that's fairly smooth and a lot of fun. For bonus enjoyment, ride the coaster at night when it lights start flashing! You can also get a video done like a music video of your ride experience afterward! If you're not a thrill rider, we highly recommend skipping this one.
Note: If you're worried about comfort, a test seat is available outside of the ride queue. This coaster also does not allow loose items, so a free-of-charge locker is available outside of the ride.

⋆ Magic Tips ⋆
The Hollywood Rip Ride Rockit allows you to choose from a list of songs by genre, but you can hack the ride to unlock additional songs. Here's how:
1. Once you've boarded, instead of selecting a song, press and hold the Rockit logo for 10 seconds until a number pad is displayed.
2. Enter one of the codes below to play your choice of bonus tracks!
   Pop: "Vogue" – Madonna (310) / "The Rainbow Connection" – The Muppets (902)
   Rock: "Break On Through" – The Doors (103) / "Crocodile Rock" – Elton John (104) / "Live" – Lenny Kravitz (115) / "Mexicola" – Queens of the Stone Age (116) / "Start Me Up" – The Rolling Stones (122) / "Run to You" – Bryan Adams (308) / "For Whom the Bell Tolls" – Metallica (703)
   R&B/Hip Hop: "I Want You Back" – The Jackson Five (302) / "Lose Yourself" – Eminem (306) / "My Everything" – Barry White (312)
Note: When you hack a song with a code, you won't be able to get a video of your ride.

TRANSFORMERS: THE RIDE 3D
Description: An explosive, 3D motion simulation ride starring the robots from the *Transformers* film series.

Perfect for: Kids, Tweens, Teens, Adults, Thrill Riders
Height Restriction: 40"
Car: 4 riders per row
Single Rider Available
Review: Join the Autobots and defeat the evil Decepticons. The ride is very similar to The Amazing Adventures of Spider-Man attraction at Islands of Adventure. However, Transformers has more realistic special effects and action sequences. It's hard not to enjoy the high-energy charm of this ride.

SHOWS AND ATTRACTIONS

MUSIC PLAZA STAGE
Description: Various stage
Perfect for: All ages
Review: Some dynamic entertainers have performed on this stage. Universal changes up the lineup and makes it even better for summer concerts. For lists of performers, check out their website **www.universalorlando.com**

STREET PERFORMERS
Look for various performances at different times around the Production Central backlot.

NEW YORK

RIDES

REVENGE OF THE MUMMY
Description: An Egyptian-themed indoor roller coaster
Perfect for: Tweens, Teens, Adults, Thrill Riders
Height Restriction: 48"
Car: 4 riders per row

Single Rider Available
Review: Face everything from eerie darkness to pyrotechnic effects as you face the wrath of an ancient mummy. This lengthy roller coaster moves through several rooms before reaching 45 miles per hour just before the climax. We won't give away the ending, but The Mummy is full of sweet revenge. Overall, the ride isn't nearly as intense as Hollywood Rip Ride Rockit, so even families can enjoy this one.
Note: *If you're worried about comfort, a test seat is available outside of the ride queue. This coaster also does not allow loose items, so a free-of-charge locker is available outside of the attraction.*

RACE THROUGH NEW YORK STARRING JIMMY FALLON
Description: 3-D Motion Simulator
Perfect for: Kids, Tweens, Teens, Adults
Height Restriction: 40"
Car: 10 riders per row
Review: Enter a façade of NBC's New York building and race through the city along with Tonight Show host, Jimmy Fallon. Filled with zany action, Race Through New York is a silly 3-D motion simulator designed as an attraction that everyone can enjoy. The queue looks very cool with decor from the Tonight Show, and the queue-less line system is interesting as well. Instead of waiting, grab a return pass at the queue, experience whichever attractions you want next, and come back during the time slot on your return pass.

Unfortunately, Race Through New York is fairly lackluster. Why, of all of its franchises, did Universal decide to create a ride around the Tonight Show? Jimmy Fallon's jokes often miss and his odd assembly of characters pale in comparison to other simulators like hilarious The Simpsons Ride. To further confuse things, guests are assigned a "group color" that is called when it's their turn to ride. Many times, this isn't properly explained in the waiting room, so employees shout at guests who shuffle into the ride wondering if they are in the correct spot. Overall, Race Through New York is a ride you probably won't care to experience twice.

SHOWS AND ATTRACTIONS

THE BLUES BROTHERS SHOW

Description: Listen to R&B jams performed live by the famous duo.

Perfect for: Adults

Length: 15 min

Review: A classic Universal attraction keeps its mark on the streets of New York. The show is very entertaining, even though the stage is small. In a way, you'll feel like you're watching the real-life Blues Brother performing right before your eyes. Perfect for classic R&B fans, though most guests may only stop for a song or two.

SAN FRANCISCO

RIDES

FAST & FURIOUS: SUPERCHARGED

Description: A 3D high-speed race simulator starring the characters from the *Fast & Furious* franchise.

Perfect for: Kids, Tweens, Teens, Adults, Thrill Riders

Height Restriction: 40" (48" without adult)

Review: Board a "party bus" on the way to an exclusive event starring the *Fast & Furious* characters as disaster strikes! While *Fast & Furious* is one of Universal's most popular franchises, the attraction doesn't quite meet up to the hype of the movies. Sure, there are cameos including Vin Diesel, the Rock, and several cool cars from the films. Fast & Furious: Supercharged unfortunately comes off like a quick and cheesy action simulator with too much build up (there are two showrooms before you actually board the ride) and not enough pay off. Overall, it's a much better overall experience than Race Through New York Starring Jimmy Fallon.

SHOWS AND ATTRACTIONS

STREET PERFORMERS

Look for singing and performing groups at various times throughout the day. Check out your map for show times on the day you arrive.

DIAGON ALLEY

THE WIZARDING WORLD
OF HARRY POTTER

RIDES

HARRY POTTER AND THE ESCAPE FROM GRINGOTTS

Description: A 3-D steel roller coaster starring characters from the *Harry Potter* film series.

Perfect for: Kids, Tweens, Teens, Adults, Thrill Riders

Height Restriction: 42"

Car: 4 riders per row

Single Rider Available

Review: Enter the cavernous vaults of Gringotts bank and ride an enchanted mine cart as you face Lord Voldemort and his evil band of Death Eaters! The visuals are stunning from the elevator that takes you into the cave-like start of the coaster. 3D glasses add to the experience as magical creatures and dark wizards attack, unleashing their fury until Harry Potter arrives to save the day!

 Escape from Gringotts is a great first ride, even from the details in the queue. While thrill riders will wish the coaster was a bit more intense, families will find the speed just right.

HOGWARTS EXPRESS

Description: A steam engine train that takes visitors from Universal Orlando to Islands of Adventure.

Perfect for: Everyone

Car: Up to 8 riders per car

Required: A Park-to-Park admission ticket

Review: Zip through the wall of Platform 9 ¾ to board the Hogwarts Express. You'll see famous characters from *Harry Potter* outside the window and even face danger in this slow moving, yet exciting attraction. We highly recommend this ride for every Harry Potter fan. Since the train links both parks, you will need a Park-to-Park admission in order to ride.

SHOWS AND ATTRACTIONS

OLLIVANDERS

Description: A brief show where the wand chooses the wizard.

Perfect for: *Harry Potter* fans of all ages

Review: Located next to the famous Ollivanders—where Harry Potter gets his wand—this show isn't to be missed by any Wizarding World fan. Garrick Ollivander, or one of his assistants, chooses one lucky person to discover their wand. Sadly, you don't get to keep the wand for free, but it is available for purchase in the next room.

· Magic Tip ·

There isn't a precise way to get chosen for Ollivanders, but from what we've noticed, participants usually near the front get chosen. Though there are always exceptions, he mostly chooses someone ages 8-20.

WAND SPOTS

Wands purchased at Ollivanders come with a map of the various practice locations around Diagon Alley. In these spots, guests can test out spells using their wands. Specific movements trigger several magical happenings. Wands work in Diagon Alley as well as Hogsmeade Village!

KNOCKTURN ALLEY
Venture if you dare, into the seedy passageways of Diagon Alley. See how wizards practice dark magic and, if you have a wand, attempt to cast some spells yourself!

THE KNIGHT BUS
Just outside of Diagon Alley is a strange, purple bus. Don't be afraid to step next to it and talk with its driver and a shrunken head.

GROGOTTS MONEY EXCHANGE
Bring in your "muggle money" and exchange it for Gringotts cash (this means bring in US currency). Not to worry because your Gringotts cash also works in Hogsmeade and Diagon Alley to purchase goods. It's also fun to interact with the grumpy goblin who exchanges your money.

CELESTINE WARBECK AND THE BANSHEES
The bewitching sensation sings her most famous tunes at various times. She's actually pretty good!

THE TALES OF BEEDLE THE BARD
Wizard and witch actors retell the tales of Beedle the Bard using stunning puppets. Kids will love this one!

FIRE-BREATHING DRAGON
The most eye-catching attraction in Diagon Alley is its resident dragon. She perches like a massive bat atop Gringotts Wizarding Bank and breathes real fire! This type of dragon is a Ukrainian Ironbelly and she's a bit finicky. Her fire seems to blast randomly, but happens about every 5-15 minutes. You'll know that she's about to blow when you hear her deep, terrifying growl (though sometimes there are false alarms). Snap a photo from the center of the alley or from the side (near the golden goblin statue) to see the entire flame at once!

WORLD EXPO

RIDES

MEN IN BLACK ALIEN ATTACK

Description: A laser-guided shooting ride
Perfect for: Young Kids, Kids, Tweens, Teens
Height Restriction: 42"
Car: 3 riders per row, 6 per vehicle
Single Rider Available
Review: Start your training as an MIB agent by blasting as many aliens as you can with your laser gun. The aliens pop out of everything from street corners to windows as you move along the city. Your score is calculated at the end. The ride is a fun for competitive people, but some of the aliens look a bit cheesy. Men in Black feels like a well-done carnival ride and we wish that it was more obvious which aliens were worth more points. However, we've figured it out and have some excellent tips—especially if you like to win!

· Magic Tips ·
Get the highest score by checking out these tips!
1. <u>Hold the Trigger</u> – Keep your finger on the trigger for continuous and rapid firing. Never let go!
2. <u>Small Means Big</u> – The smaller the alien, the bigger the score. Look for hidden aliens popping out of windows and trashcans. They are worth far more than their big brothers.
3. <u>Keep Shooting</u> – Lock on to little targets for as long as you can! You can shoot a target more than once.
4. <u>Time the Bonus</u> – There is a 100,000-point bonus at the end of the ride. Look for the enormous, room-sized bug and listen for Agent Zed to say "Push the Red Button!" Press the button on the dash in front of you and hit it as soon as he says "push". Don't let go of the bonus button and multiple people in your car can get it, too!

SHOWS AND ATTRACTIONS

FEAR FACTOR LIVE
Description: An audience interactive stunt show
Perfect for: Thrill Riders who want to participate
Length: 20 min
Review: Fear Factor Live allows visitors to audition for various stunts like jumping over cars and reaching into a tank of live eels. While it may be fun for participants to watch, audience members are often bored and unamused by the flat jokes and dull stunts. When a winner is crowned, everyone is ready for the show to be over already.

⋆ **Magic Tip** ⋆
If you'd like to audition—and are 18 or older—head to the kiosk in front of Fear Factor at least 70 minutes before your choice of show time. Fear Factor may only run seasonally.

SPRINGFIELD

HOME OF THE SIMPSONS

RIDES

THE SIMPSONS RIDE
Description: Motion-simulation ride starring characters from *The Simpsons*
Perfect for: Tweens, Teens, Adults
Height Restriction: 40"
Car: 4 riders per row, 8 per vehicle
Review: One of the funniest rides in the world, *The Simpsons* delivers edgy, top-quality amusement. Join Homer, Bart, Marge, Lisa, Maggie, Grampa, and the rest of Springfield as Sideshow Bob threatens to destroy Krustyland. The ride is 2D, though the characters have been rendered with 3D animation for a more

immersive feel. When waiting in the queue, read as many signs as you can, as they are all filled with hilarious quips and digs at amusement park clichés.

KANG AND KODOS' TWIRL 'N' HURL
Description: Motion simulation ride starring characters from The Simpsons.
Perfect for: Young Kids and Kids
Height Restriction: None
Car: 2 riders per saucer
Review: *The Simpsons* meets Dumbo the Flying Elephant ride in this classic spin around kid-friendly attraction. Despite the ride's name, this ride is rather slow-paced and aimed at families with young kids. Adults will get a kick out of the sound bites ripped straight from The Simpsons, though all of the humor is suitable for kids.

WOODY WOODPECKER'S KIDZONE

RIDES

E. T. ADVENTURE
Description: Ride flying bikes to help save E. T. and his home planet.
Perfect for: Families
Height Restriction: None
Car: 4 riders per row
Review: The magic of E. T. is brought to life with animatronics and rideable flying bicycles. If you've experienced Peter Pan's Flight at Disney, it's a bit like that. However, we get mixed reviews from this attraction. Tweens, teens, and young adults will likely find the ride heavily outdated. Yet, kids will love visiting E.T.'s home planet and parents will enjoy the overall nostalgia.

WOODY WOODPECKER'S NUTHOUSE COASTER

Description: An outdoor "junior coaster" designed for families with kids
Perfect for: Families
Height Restriction: None
Car: 2 riders per row
Review: Ride around on Woody Woodpecker's train coaster. It's slow-paced and a lot of fun for kids looking for something thrilling for them to experience.

SHOWS AND ATTRACTIONS

ANIMAL ACTORS ON LOCATION

Description: A stage show starring talented animals
Perfect for: Families
Length: 20 Minutes
Review: Live animals take over a stage and show audiences their natural talents. There are tons of laughs for families with kids. Watch birds soar, dogs perform tricks, and maybe even hear a pig hilariously snorting. At the end of the show, the trainers may allow audience members to pet some of the animals.

FIEVEL'S PLAYLAND

A water playground inspired by *An American Tail* and *Fievel Goes West* animated films. Kids might not know the stories, but they'll love the water slide!

A DAY IN THE PARK WITH BARNEY

Description: A stage show starring Barney the purple dinosaur.
Perfect for: Young Kids
Length: 30 Minutes
Review: Barney and his friends sing songs and play games in a stage designed like a happy park. Young kids will love singing along and the silly fun. After the show, kids can play with Barney in an outdoor playground.

CURIOUS GEORGE GOES TO TOWN

A brightly colored playground straight out of the Curious George book series. It's famous for splash areas and things to climb. Perfect for parents who need a break and kids who have a lot of energy.

HOLLYWOOD

SHOWS AND ATTRACTIONS

UNIVERSAL ORLANDO'S HORROR MAKE-UP SHOW

Description: Learn how Hollywood make-up artists create movie monsters

Perfect for: Tweens, Teens, Adults

Review: Horror movies come to life in this unique Hollywood make-up show. While there are more laughs than screams, it still may be too scary for young kids.

UNIVERSAL'S SUPERSTAR PARADE

Description: See parade floats starring the characters from *Despicable Me*, SpongeBob SquarePants, Dora the Explorer, and many more!

Perfect for: Young Kids, Kids, Tweens

Review: Line up early on the streets of Hollywood to see these floats go by. Some of the pieces are very intricate, but the characters bring this show to life. If your kids are dying to see some fun characters, this is the show to attend. We recommend getting to the parade 20 minutes prior. Check the map for times.

Bring your American Express credit card to the Brown Derby Hat shop before the start of the parade and gain access to an exclusive viewing area. You must get to the shop at least 15 minutes before the parade time. Seating is first come, first served.

UNIVERSAL ORLANDO'S CINEMATIC CELEBRATION
Description: A fantastic nighttime water show with special effects and characters from *Jurassic World*, *Harry Potter*, *Despicable Me* and more.
Perfect for: Everyone
Review: This stunning, 20-minute water show brings movies alive with music and projections on water fountains in the center lagoon. Scenes from popular film franchises are projected onto the water with music and colors. This effect looks a bit like the Bellagio Fountains in Las Vegas or the World of Color show at the Disneyland Resort in California. We highly recommend planning this show as a conclusion to your day.

CHAPTER SIX

UNIVERSAL'S ISLANDS OF ADVENTURE

THEMED AREAS

Islands of Adventure creates fantastic worlds based around popular franchises. From Marvel Comics and Harry Potter to Jurassic Park and Dr. Seuss, there's something for everyone at Islands of Adventure! The lands aren't actually islands placed in the middle of water. Instead, the stunning landscaping and center lake give the feeling of distinct and unique worlds separated by a body of water.

Port of Entry

A hodgepodge of world bazaars that will make you feel like Aladdin or Indiana Jones might live there. The Port of Entry is a fun, shop-filled starting area before you step into the islands.

Marvel Super Hero Island

Islands of Adventure does justice to comic books by bringing Spider-Man, the Hulk, X-Men, and other superheroes to life in this colorful area. These aren't the newer versions of Marvel's creations, but more the 80's and 90's comic book style. Thrill riders will love the high-speed Hulk Coaster and everyone will enjoy the action-packed Amazing Adventures of Spider-Man.

Note: *But, doesn't Disney own Marvel? Yes, they do, but Universal acquired the rights before Disney acquired the brand.*

Seuss Landing

The bright, cheerful world of Dr. Seuss awaits guests in this island designed for young kids. See The Cat in the Hat, try green eggs and ham, and ride above Circus McGurkus on a train. One of the coolest features of Seuss Landing are the wacky palm trees that were picked for their naturally bent trunks.

Toon Lagoon

Splash into the world of classic cartoons like Pop Eye, Dudley Do-Right, and Betty Boop in this surprising island. Toon Lagoon might get shadowed out by Harry Potter and Marvel, but it's water-based attractions and attention to detail are some of the park's best.

The Lost Continent

Before Harry Potter took over, The Lost Continent was the largest island. Though its number of attractions has been significantly reduced, since Harry Potter this mythology-themed island still has some stunning sights and delicious eats. The Lost Continent is the only island not themed after an existing franchise.

Hogsmeade – The Wizarding World of Harry Potter

The magic of *Harry Potter* comes to life in this wizard-themed wonderland. With snow-capped buildings, enchanted storefronts, and unique attractions, *Harry Potter* fans may never want to leave. Guests can enter Hogwarts castle and purchase wands that interact with areas of Hogsmeade and Diagon Alley. Though Hogsmeade is often crowded, this island is not to be missed!

Jurassic Park

This tropical-feeling island is perfectly set as an homage to the *Jurassic Park* film series. Meet velociraptors or plunge down the river cruise after escaping a giant T-Rex. There are also many attractions for kids at the Jurassic Park Discovery center and Camp Jurassic playground.

Skull Island

Based around Peter Jackson's *King Kong* film, this island houses one attraction: Reign of Kong. The creepy exterior of this island is filled with black rock and human skulls.

MARVEL SUPER HERO ISLAND

RIDES

THE INCREDIBLE HULK
Description: A fast-launching steel roller coaster with loops
Type: Roller Coaster
Perfect for: Thrill Riders
Height Restriction: 54"
Car: 4 riders in each row
Single Rider Available
Review: The Incredible Hulk roller coaster has been revamped in 2016 to include a new storyline and special effects. Prepare for 7 loops, high speeds, and a lot of thrilling fun! In our opinion, The Hulk Coaster is one of the best.
Note: The ride does not permit loose items such as hats, sunglasses, or cell phones in pockets. A metal detector scans guests before riding, so make sure you put these items in a free locker near the roller coaster before riding. Free lockers are time sensitive and only hold your items for the duration of your ride.

STORM FORCE ACCELATRON
Description: A spinning ride similar to Disney's tea cups
Perfect for: Kids, Tweens
Height Restriction: None
Car: Up to 4 riders per cup
Review: Battle Magneto alongside Storm from X-men. Storm Force is dizzying fun for families with kids—and strong stomachs. Riders control the speed of the spinning by turning a wheel.

THE AMAZING ADVENTURES OF SPIDER-MAN
Description: A 3-D motion simulation ride with a moving car
Perfect for: Kids, Tweens, Teens, Adults, Thrill Riders
Height Restriction: 40"
Car: 4 riders per row
Single Rider Available

Review: Grab your 3D glasses for this motion simulator based around the many of adventures of Spider-Man. Combat villains like Dr. Octopus and Hobgoblin as you race through New York City. This ride is great fun for everyone with its unique style of large screens and a moving vehicle—only the Transformers ride feels very similar.

DOCTOR DOOM'S FEARFALL
Description: An 18-story freefall ride
Perfect for: Thrill Riders
Height Restriction: 52"
Car: 4 riders per row
Single Rider Available
Review: Try and calm your nerves before facing Dr. Doom's revenge for you and The Fantastic Four. Smoke, lights, and a massive drop will make any heart race! Basically, a glorified carnival ride, but still a lot of fun. While you're at the top, there's an amazing view of the park. But what goes up must come down. We only recommend this heart-racing ride for thrill riders.

SHOWS AND ATTRACTIONS

MARVEL HEROES
Look out for members of the Avengers and the X-Men as they walk or drive through Marvel Super Hero Island. There are also meet ups with Spider-Man, Wolverine, Captain America, and other famous superheroes.

SEUSS LANDING

RIDES

THE CAT IN THE HAT
Description: A slow-paced ride starring The Cat in the Hat
Type: Dark Ride
Perfect for: Kids
Height Restriction: 36"
Car: 2-3 riders in each row
Review: Hop aboard a slow-moving car that takes you through the story of The Cat in the Hat. Families with kids under 10 will love the colorful scenes and crazy animatronics. Actually, *any* Dr. Seuss fan will find this ride very charming.

THE HIGH IN THE SKY SEUSS TROLLEY TRAIN RIDE
Description: A slow-moving train that winds around Seuss Landing
Perfect for: Families
Height Restriction: 40"
Car: 2 riders per row
Review: Travel over the low buildings of Seuss Landing on this colorful train. It's a nice time if you'll looking for a break, as the lines are rarely long. However, not much happens other than some sights that you can see from down below.

CARO-SEUSS-EL
Description: A Dr. Seuss-themed carousel
Perfect for: Young Kids and Kids
Height Restriction: None
Car: 1 rider per "horse"
Review: Hop on bobbing yaks, elephants, and other Seuss-drawn creatures. Another well-detailed ride designed for families with young kids.

ONE FISH, TWO FISH, RED FISH, BLUE FISH

Description: A fish-themed ride like Dumbo the Flying Elephant at Disneyland and The Magic Kingdom
Perfect for: Young Kids and Kids
Height Restriction: None
Car: 2 riders per fish
Review: Gently soar above the water on your choice of primary-colored fish. Control how high—or how low—your fish goes! Young kids will especially love this attraction.

SHOWS AND ATTRACTIONS

OH THE STORIES YOU'LL HEAR

Description: Live stage show
Perfect for: Families
Review: Listen to stories told by Dr. Seuss characters. Look for The Cat in the Hat, Thing 1 and Thing 2, and even the grumpy Grinch! The theatre is outdoors, but the seating area is shaded. This is perfect for families who need a break and want to watch a show.

IF I RAN THE ZOO

A hedge maze with interactive walls and water play areas. There aren't any real animals in this zoo, but kids 10 and under will love to cool off in this colorful play area.

TOON LAGOON

RIDES

POPEYE AND BLUTO'S BILGE-RAT BARGES

Description: A water rapids raft ride with the characters from Popeye cartoons
Type: River rapids raft ride

Perfect for: Kids, Tweens, Teens, Adults
Height Restriction: 42"
Car: 12 riders per raft with seats in pairs of 2
Review: Rush down a raging rapid on rafts as Popeye and Bluto battle for Olive Oyl's attention. This is one of the best rapids rides we've ever experienced with its comical humor and cartoon design. Be prepared because you *will* get wet! We recommend experiencing this attraction in the middle of the day when the sun is shining to help you dry off.

DUDLEY DO-RIGHT'S RIPSAW FALLS
Description: A log water ride starring characters from Rocky and Bullwinkle's Dudley Do-Right cartoon
Perfect for: Kids, Tweens, Teens, Adults
Height Restriction: 44"
Car: 5 riders per log
Review: Journey through the wacky tale of Canada's cartoon Mountie on a log raft fit for 5. At the end, you'll plunge down a 7 story waterfall. We love Dudley Do-Right's Ripsaw Falls for the beautiful decorations, and comedy. This attraction is especially popular in the summer, so visit just before noon to avoid the longer lines. You will get wet, but likely not nearly as soaked as Popeye and Bluto's Bilge-Rat Barges.

SHOWS AND ATTRACTIONS

ME SHIP, THE OLIVE
Popeye's 3-story ship and water play area. If you don't want to get soaked on the raft ride, there are water cannons on Me Ship, The Olive where you can take aim at riders while staying dry. Kids ages 10 and under will enjoy this play area the most.

THE LOST CONTINENT

SHOWS AND ATTRACTIONS

POSEIDON'S FURY

Description: A special effects theatre show in a cave
Perfect for: Kids, Tweens, and Teens
Length: 15 minutes
Review: The Olympian God, Poseidon, unleashes his aquatic wrath on all those who intrude his ancient ruins. Hokey comedy and special effects make this show a cool first watch. Kids and tweens will likely love it and teens will find it fine. However, the outdated special effects and drawn-out storyline might bore adults. Still, we think it's worth seeing if you're looking for an indoor show that's out of the heat.

THE MYSTICAL FOUNTAIN

A sassy fountain that interacts with guests walking close to it. Step too close and you might get sprayed!

SKULL ISLAND

RIDES

SKULL ISLAND: REIGN OF KONG

Description: A 3D journey into the island ruled by the giant gorilla, King Kong
Type: 3D simulation ride
Perfect for: Tweens, Teens, and Adults
Height Restriction: 36"
Car: 6 riders per row

Review: Step into a dark, foreboding temple that houses a fierce, massive gorilla. A safari truck takes you into Kong's world where dinosaurs and giant spiders might attack at any moment. The ride is divided into segments including one with a 3-D screen that domes over the caravan. In the queue, there are a few spooky surprises as well. At the end, prepare to face Kong himself. This ride may be too terrifying for young kids.

HOGSMEADE VILLAGE

THE WIZARDING WORLD OF HARRY POTTER

RIDES

HARRY POTTER AND THE FORBIDDEN JOURNEY
Description: An adventure ride starring the characters of the *Harry Potter* films
Type: Simulation ride
Perfect for: Kids, Tweens, Teens, and Adults
Height Restriction: 48"
Car: 4 riders per row
Single Rider Available
Review: Enter the magnificent Hogwarts castle and meet Harry Potter characters in the various rooms. Look for enchanted portraits, magic spells, a winding garden, and stunning artwork.
The queue is just as entertaining as the ride. Once you board a specialized crane-like vehicle, you'll fly through Hogwarts to encounter a game of Quidditch, a run-away dragon, spitting spiders, and even soul-sucking Dementors. Harry Potter and the Forbidden Journey is one of the most unique rides in the world, and not to be missed!
Note: *If you're worried about your comfort on the ride, a test seat is available before the queue.*

FLIGHT OF THE HIPPOGRIFF
Description: An outdoor, family-friendly roller coaster
Type: Junior Roller coaster
Perfect for: Young Kids, Kids, Tweens
Height Restriction: 36"
Car: 2 riders per row
Review: A hippogriff is half eagle, half horse and very moody. Hagrid, the groundskeeper at Hogwarts castle, once had a hippogriff named Buckbeak who befriends Harry Potter. This ride is inspired by that creature. Flight of the Hippogriff is a great introductory roller coaster for kids who need a stepping stone to the bigger coasters. Though the ride is just over a minute in length, the track is smooth and fun for the whole family.
Note: The seats on this ride are designed for kids, so taller and larger guests may not sit comfortably in them. Unfortunately, Flight of the Hippogriff does not offer a test seat.

FORBDIDEN FOREST ROLLER COASTER
Description: A both indoor and outdoor roller coaster set to open in the Fall of 2019.
Type: Roller coaster
Perfect for: Kids, Tweens, Teens, Adults, Thrill Riders
Height Restriction: TBA
Car: TBA
Review: Universal has yet to announce details about this new attraction, but our observations of the construction show the outline of the Forbidden Forest near Hogsmeade Village. Show buildings also foreshadow a coaster that hugs close to the ground and winds in and out of spaces with potential special effect scenes! We'll update with details about this attraction on our free e-mail newsletter. Subscribe today: **www.magicguidebooks.com/list**

HOGWARTS EXPRESS
Travel between Islands of Adventure and Universal Studios on the famous train from Harry Potter. You'll need a park-to-park ticket to ride. The experiences are different, depending if you travel to or from Hogsmeade. For more details about the Hogwarts Express, see Diagon Alley in the Universal Studios chapter.

SHOWS AND ATTRACTIONS

OLLIVANDERS

Description: A brief show where the wand chooses the wizard.

Perfect for: Harry Potter fans of all ages

Review: Located next to the famous Ollivanders—where Harry Potter gets his wand—this show isn't to be missed by any Wizarding World fan. Garrick Ollivander, or one of his assistants, invites a lucky park guest to take part of the wand selection experience. Sadly, you don't get to keep the wand that chooses you, but they are available for purchase in the next room.

⋅ **Magic Tip** ⋅

There isn't a surefire way to be chosen by Ollivander, but from what we've noticed, participants are usually in near the front and to his right get picked the most. Though there are always exceptions, he mostly chooses guests ages 8-20.

WAND SPOTS

Wands purchased at Ollivanders come with a map of the various magic practice locations around Hogsmeade Village. In these spots, guests can test spells by moving their wand in specific directions. These movements trigger several magical happenings around Hogsmeade Village and Diagon Alley.

THE FROG CHOIR

See Hogwarts students and their singing toads perform songs from the wizarding world. The singers are talented and the show runs about 10 minutes.

TRIWIZARD SPIRIT RALLY

See wizard students from foreign wizarding schools, Durmstrang and Beauxbatons, show their school spirit with dazzling choreographed routines. The show runs about 5 minutes and is a lot of fun to watch while sipping on Butterbeer.

THE NIGHTTIME LIGHTS AT HOGWARTS CASTLE

One of the best shows at Universal Orlando is projected onto the Hogwarts Castle on select nights. This brief, 5-minute show runs about every 20 minutes in front of the castle. However, viewing it may be difficult due to limited space. We recommend getting a times guide when you enter the park (near the maps) and arriving 30 minutes before showtime. The best viewing spots are near Flight of the Hippogriff!

FORBIDDEN FOREST ATTRACTIONS
Universal has promised several new and exciting Harry Potter attractions in the Forbidden Forest scheduled to open by Fall of 2019. Expect new locations to use your wand and greets with forest-dwelling fantastic creatures!

JURASSIC PARK

RIDES

JURASSIC PARK RIVER ADVENTURE
Description: A water-based boat ride with dinosaurs and an 85-foot drop
Type: Boat ride
Perfect for: Thrill Riders
Height Restriction: 42"
Car: 4 riders per row
Review: A boat ride that begins with gentle, animatronic giants and concludes with attacking carnivores. Drift calmly at first until the raptors and T-Rex show their teeth, then get ready for the big, eight-story fall! You'll likely get wet, but it'll be worth it because Jurassic Park River Adventure is one of the best rides in Islands of Adventure!

PTERANODON FLYERS
Description: High-flying kids' gliders on a track
Type: Track glider
Perfect for: Kids
Height Restriction: 36" minimum (under 48" must have guardian ride, too)
Car: 2 riders per glider

Review: Kids soar around Jurassic Park island on these high-up tracked gliders. Pteranodon Flyers have a limited rider occupancy, so lines often back up. Luckily, Universal started a Virtual Line for this attraction. A kiosk in front of the ride distributes return times so your kids can have fun in the playground instead of waiting in a long line.

Note: *Since this attraction is designed for kids, adults must have a child between 36" and 48" with them to ride.*

SHOWS AND ATTRACTIONS

RAPTOR ENCOUNTER

Visit the Jurassic World Raptor Paddock and meet Blue the velociraptor. A "keeper" will tell you about raptor behaviors and you can even pose for a terrifying photo with her! Lines can be a bit long for this short attraction.

CAMP JURASSIC

An outdoor play area for kids to run, play, swing, and jump. The design is like an archeological dig site where kids can squirt each other with water cannons and play in giant nets surrounded by lush trees.

JURASSIC PARK DISCOVERY CENTER

Enter the famous visitors center of Jurassic Park. See giant model dinosaurs, egg incubators, and several hands-on learning activities.

CHAPTER SEVEN

UNIVERSAL'S VOLCANO BAY
WATER PARK

INTRODUCTION

In 2017, Universal Orlando Resort opened a world-class water park styled after a Polynesian island. Volcano Bay centers around an active "volcano" that steams and houses several unique water slides. Filled with fun for young kids and thrill seekers alike, Volcano Bay lives up to Universal's aspiration for a third theme park.

Note: Some of the slides have height and weight restrictions that will prevent some from riding.

TAPUTAPU

Volcano Bay does things differently than Universal Studios and Islands of Adventure. Most of the rides are "queue-less" meaning that you don't have to wait in a physical line to board your desired attraction. Instead, you are given a special waterproof bracelet called a TapuTapu. By scanning your bracelet on special totems near the slides, you'll have your wait time held for you. Your bracelet (which sort of looks like an old school Tamagotchi) will buzz when it's your turn to return to the slide. In the meantime, you can walk around the park and ride other water slides, lounge, eat, float in the lazy river — or do whatever else your heart desires.

Here's What the TapuTapu Does...

1. Virtual Queue – Holds your place in line without having to actually wait in a queue
2. Locker – Store your belongings in a locker starting at $8 (prices may change) and use TapuTapu as a key
3. Photo Spots – Takes special photos near choice spots and can e-mail them to you
4. Explosions – Scan your bracelet at special spots around the Kopiko Wai Winding River and other attractions to cue explosions or control water cannons

Notes: When you first try the TapuTapu bracelet, its functionality may feel confusing, especially on crowded days. It takes about an hour to get the hang of it, so get there at park open if you can, before the crowd rush, and start experimenting with the TapuTapu.

WHAT TO BRING

The water parks have nearly everything you'll need for poolside-fun — but with a cost. That's why we recommend bringing these items with you into the parks:

1. Sunscreen – You'll be out in the sun all day, after all
2. Beach towels – Rentals are available
3. Change of clothing – It's not required, but we recommend it if you plan to go somewhere afterward

⋆ Magic Tips ⋆

1. Volcano Bay does not allow glass, food, coolers, your own rafts, or life vests into the park (they provide complimentary life vests if needed).
2. You also cannot wear shoes onto the rides, though rash guards and water shirts are allowed.
3. If you wear sunglasses, be careful not to lose them on a water slide!

CABANAS AND LOUNGERS

Looking for a reserved spot out of the sun? Volcano Bay's Cabanas are a perfect addition for your trip. Starting at $29.99, you and your family can enjoy a reserved spot in the shade.

Padded Lounger – Rent two premium loungers with a built-in locker for your belongings. The loungers also have covers for your face. At $29.99, per day (plus tax), this is a great deal — especially since you won't have to pay extra for a locker!

Single Cabana – A private, shaded lounge area for up to 6 people. Starts at $159.99 per day, plus tax.

Family Suite Cabanas – Made for up to 16 people in a spacious cabana area. Prices start at $299.99 per day, plus tax.

THEMED AREAS

Volcano Bay is broken up into 4 themed areas. These aren't as drastic in theme as the "dry" parks like Universal Studios and Islands of Adventure. However, they each serve their purpose to deliver thrills or fun splashes for the kids.

Wave Village – Hit the waves or relax on the sand in this seaside simulated beach

Krakatau – Located inside of the volcano with thrilling slides

River Village – Sail along on a raft though a lazy river or have fun with your kids in a reef specially designed for them

Rainforest Village – A collection of family-friendly and thrilling slides

KRAKATAU

ATTRACTIONS

KRAKATAU AQUA COASTER

Description: Slide up and down hills around the active volcano in this popular water slide.

Type: Solo tube slide

Perfect for: Families, Tweens, Teens, Thrill Riders

Review: A unique water slide designed like a roller coaster. Ride with your family or group over hills on a toboggan-like raft. The thrill of this ride can be enjoyable to most.

Height Restriction: 42" minimum (under 48" must ride with adult)

˙ Magic Tip ˙

On busier days, this ride can have extremely long wait times. We recommend riding it first.

KALA AND TA NUI SEPENTINE BODY SLIDES

Description: Plunge down the volcano after a trap door opens beneath you!

Type: Solo tube slide

Perfect for: Thrill Riders

Height Restriction: 48" minimum, 230 lbs. maximum weight

Review: An intense plunge into core of the volcano. For thrill riders, this is a must. Everyone else might want to stay clear! This is the less intense version of the Ko'okiri Body Plunge.

Note: We cover our noses as we go onto this attraction to avoid getting water up there!

KO'OKIRI BODY PLUNGE

Description: The dreaded red-colored tube! Stand on a trap door before it opens and send you plummeting at a 70 degree angle!

Type: Solo tube slide

Perfect for: Thrill Riders

Height Restriction: 48" minimum, 300 lbs. maximum weight
Review: An intense plunge straight into core of the volcano. Certainly the most intense slide in the park! We only recommend the Body Plunge for thrill riders.
Note: Like the Body Slides, we cover our noses on this attraction.

PUNGA RACERS
Description: Race your friends down the hill as you grab hold of your slippery mat.
Type: Water mat racing slide
Perfect for: Kids, Tweens, Teens, Adults, Thrill Riders
Height Restriction: 42" minimum (under 48" must ride with adult)
Review: Unlike other mat racing waterslides, this ride can feel a little rocky if you don't completely still, and it's hard to gauge where the other racers are. However, we like that the mats have handles to grip as you go. Ultimately, we feel that the Tween crowd will like this slide the best for its competitive and unique nature.

WAVE VILLAGE

ATTRACTIONS

WATURI BEACH
Description: A wave pool in front of the volcano
Type: Wave pool
Perfect for: Kids, Tweens, Teens, Adults
Height Restriction: Kids under 48" are required to wear a life vest (these are provided by Volcano Bay)
Review: Wade in this pool until the drums start to bang—then get ready for the rush of waves! We only recommend this attraction for strong swimmers unless they keep in the shallow areas. Kids to teens seem to love Waturi Beach the most.

THE REEF
Description: A calmer wave pool in front of the volcano
Type: Wave pool
Perfect for: Kids, Adults
Height Restriction: Kids under 48" are required to wear a life vest (these are provided by Volcano Bay)
Review: If the waters of Waturi Beach are too strong, but you like the splash of the waves, head to The Reef and enjoy a calmer experience.

RIVER VILLAGE

ATTRACTIONS

KOPIKO WAI WINDING RIVER
Description: A lazy river that winds throughout Volcano Bay
Type: Lazy river
Perfect for: Kids, Tweens, Teens, Adults
Height Restriction: None
Review: A gentle stream through caves and open air around the water park. Even better if you grab an inner tube and just let the current take you!
· Magic Tip ·
Look for TapTu Play zones around the lazy river. Here you can scan your TapuTapu bracelet and shoot water cannons or spray at the people in the river!

HONU IKA MOANA
Description: Board a round raft and surf the waves on this massive tube.
Type: Group raft water slide
Perfect for: Kids, Tweens, Teens, Adults, Thrill Riders
Height Restriction: 42" minimum (under 48" must ride with adult)

Review: Based on a legend of islanders who rode whales and sea turtles in the Pacific, you'll cruise over giant crested waves on these thrilling water raft rides.

KID ATTRACTIONS

TOT TIKI REEF*
A collection of slides and splash zones designed for young kids.

RUNAMUKKA REEF*
An outdoor water play fortress

Note: These areas are designed for Kids under 48"

RAINFOREST VILLAGE

ATTRACTIONS

MAKU PUIHI ROUND RAFT RIDES
Description: A group raft water slides
Type: Group raft water slides
Perfect for: Kids, Tweens, Teens, Adults, Thrill Riders
Height Restriction: 42" minimum (under 48" must ride with adult)
Review: Large water slides with giant rafts big enough to hold a group of six!

TANIWHA TUBES
Description: Ride singles or doubles in this tube slide
Type: Raft water slides
Perfect for: Kids, Tweens, Teens, Adults, Thrill Riders
Height Restriction: 42" minimum (under 48" must ride with adult)

Review: Located at the edge of Volcano Bay, these fun tube slides typically have short wait times.

OHYA AND OHNO DROP SLIDES
Description: Fast water slides with a plunge
Type: Solo water slides
Perfect for: Kids, Tweens, Teens, Adults, Thrill Riders
Height Restriction: 48" minimum
Review: Slip, slide, and plunge out of these high-speed water slides designed for single riders without rafts.

TEWAWA THE FEARLESS RIVER
A faster version of the lazy river perfect for floating on a tube. Must be 42" to enter. Kids under 48" are required to wear a life vest (these are provided by Volcano Bay)

PUKA ULI LAGOON
A large pool with splashing water jets designed for relaxing.

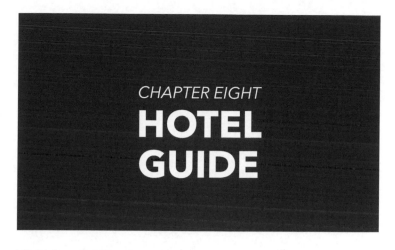

CHAPTER EIGHT

HOTEL GUIDE

INTRODUCTION

The Universal Orlando Resort has six uniquely stylized hotels within its property. Whether you're looking for an inexpensive, but great place to stay with your family or something a bit high-end and relaxing, at least one of these hotels is a great fit. Expect friendly staff, clean rooms, and beautiful pools in every location.

· Magic Tip ·

The larger resorts can often feel very spread out. Sometimes it's a bit of a trek from the front to your room. To solve this issue, we always recommend that you request a room closer to the amenities. Some resorts also have "preferred" rooms placed closer to the lobby and pool for an additional cost.

HOTEL CLASSIFICATIONS

Premier Hotel – Luxury. These hotels are closest in proximity to the theme parks, CityWalk and amenities.

Preferred Hotel – Deluxe. A bit further away, but water taxis and shuttle buses get you there for free.

Prime Value Hotel – Affordable. Not very close to the parks, but still a great value with free shuttles to the attractions and CityWalk. These are often close to Volcano Bay.

AMENITIES

All Universal Orlando Resort hotels come with the following perks for their guests:

Early Park Admission

Beat the crowds and enter the parks an hour before regular opening times. You'll need a paid admission for entry.

Transportation

Get free transport to CityWalk and the theme parks via water taxi or shuttle. You just need one room key for you and your party to ride. These transports run every 15-20 minutes. The water taxis are the best (and most fun) way to travel throughout the resort. Hop aboard one of these boats to see lush surroundings and the skippers are great at answering questions about your visit. No need to tip the captain, but you can if you'd like. The shuttle system are busses that run from hotels to the entrance of the park by the normal roads. You won't get in as close as the water taxis, which drop off in front of the parks and CityWalk, but the busses are completely free to guests.

Room Key Charging

You can add your credit card to your room key for easy charging. Just ask the front desk when you check in for this option. Or add your credit card to your room key via the Universal Orlando application. Much better than carrying around loads of plastic cards!

Free Merchandise Delivery

If you see something you'd like to buy in CityWalk or one of the parks, you don't have to carry it around with you all day. Before purchasing, ask a sales clerk if the item is available for room delivery. Most of the shops within the theme parks and CityWalk have this option.

Exclusive Character Appearances

See your favorite Universal characters up-close and exclusively available to resort hotel guests. Ask your hotel concierge for details on appearances, as the locations and characters may chance.

Golf Universal Orlando

A free shuttle to the Grand Cypress Golf Club in Orlando, about 15 minutes southwest of the resort, closer to Disney World. These full, green courses come with complimentary clubs and golf balls to use.

MORE AMENITIES

Guests of the Hard Rock Hotel, Loews Portofino Bay Hotel, and Loews Royal Pacific Resort can enjoy the following:

Free Universal Express Unlimited

One of the better reasons to pay top dollar for these hotels, Express Unlimited allows you to skip the lines to nearly every attraction in both parks. You'll still need to purchase a park ticket for admission to use Express Unlimited.

Priority Restaurant Seating

Many guests don't use this feature, but you should! If you didn't get a restaurant reservation, make sure to tell the host/hostess that you are staying at one of these three hotels, and the host will move your place earlier.

HOTEL PARKING

$27 for self-parking
$36 for valet
$29 day-only guest parking
$41 day-only guest valet

HARD ROCK HOTEL

Best for: Everyone
Theme: Rock and roll in a California mission oasis
Cost: $$$–$$$$
Location: 5-minute walking distance to parks and CityWalk
Review: The Hard Rock is our favorite hotel in the parks for its location, friendly staff, stylized and comfortable rooms, large pool area, and superb dining. Rock 'n' roll memorabilia garnish the lobby and some of the rooms. Outside, look for palms, green grass, and a fountain with guitars near the entrance. Guests of this hotel have access to all amenities including free Universal Express Unlimited and priority restaurant seating. Walking distance to CityWalk's nightlife and the fun of the parks, the hotel is closer to the Universal Studios side than Islands of Adventure. Though Hard Rock is usually the most expensive hotel at Universal—and often sells out during busy months—you can get a discount by booking as early as possible.

ROOMS & SUITES

Every room in the Hard Rock is well-decorated and stylish. You'll often have a choice between a king or two queen beds. Rooms usually have an option for a rollaway bed.

Standard Rooms – 375 sq. ft., sleeps up to 5 guests. Views are often without much scenery, like a parking lot or rooftop.

Garden View Room – 375 sq. ft., sleeps up to 5 guests. Views are of the green, tropical garden.

Pool Room – 375 sq. ft., sleeps up to 5 guests. Your room will look out to the pool. We recommend this view as Hard Rock's pool is stunning.

Deluxe King Rooms – 400 sq. ft. sleeps up to 3 guests. These rooms also come with a sitting area for lounging.

Deluxe Queen Rooms – 500 sq. ft. sleeps up to 5 guests. If you are hosting a larger party, go with this room so that you'll have more space to stretch out than a standard queen room.

Kids Suites – 800 sq. ft. and sleeps up to 5 guests. If you are looking for more space for your family, this a great option. There is a king bed for parents in one room and twin beds for kids in the next. The kids room also comes with smaller sized furniture for them. Overall, we don't feel these rooms are as well decorated as others, but they are very practical.

King Suites – 650 sq. ft. and sleeps up to 3 guests. The King bed is on one half and the connecting "entertainment room" with sofa and television, is on the other. You can connect up to 3 rooms, including 2 King Suites, to sleep up to 13 guests. All of these suites come with a garden or pool view, depending on your choice.

Hospitality Suites – 1,250 sq. ft. space designed for entertaining guests. Equipped with a full kitchen and dining area, these aren't rooms so much for sleeping as they are for meetings. However, the Hospitality Suite does sleep up to 4 guests with a king bed and a roll away bed. Unfortunately, there aren't hospitality suites with two queen beds.

Graceland Suite – 2,000 sq. ft. and sleeps 2. If you're looking to impress, the Graceland Suite is the best room on the resort. It houses large televisions, a lounge, fire place, marble shower, whirlpool tub, walk-in closet, and even a baby grand piano. Celebrities often stay in this suite so the lavishness is meant to meet top standards. We think the Graceland Suite is awesome if you're okay with spending top dollar, but for large parties, book connecting rooms instead, as this space is just meant for a couple.

Club – Access to an exclusive area with water, snacks, breakfast bites, beer, wine, and sometimes vodka mixers for adults 21 and older. The club rooms are located on a higher level and range from standard rooms without views to suites with gorgeous views. You can also request a 2-bedroom on the club level, which would be a king suite attached to a room with two queen beds.

AMENITIES

Pool – Kids and adults love Hard Rock's pool! Designed like a desert oasis, this massive pool has several hot tubs, a water slide, and even a beach-like area. At night, watch kid-friendly movies and order dining from the Beachclub bar. Hard Rock's pool is fairly shallow and mostly for wading, which is ideal for families and adults just looking to cool off. Of course, no pool oasis is complete without numerous lounge chairs and wait service, which Hard Rock perfectly delivers.

Body Rock Fitness Center – Get a workout at this hotel's complimentary gym. Equipped with treadmills, bicycles, elliptical, free weights, and a stairmaster, the room isn't enormous, but it gets the job done for a vacation pump. The fitness center also maps out jogging paths up to 3 miles around the property and houses a locker room with saunas.

Business Center – Print, copy, fax, mail, and e-mail from this all-in-one self-service room. The business center is open 24 hours, 7 days a week, and is very helpful. Some of the items may cost to use, see concierge desk for details.

Mandara Spa – Located in the Loews Portofino Bay Hotel, the spa isn't very close to the Hard Rock, but it is relaxing. Prepare to spend $150 or more on a massage, though it does offer a set of other services from skincare to body treatments.

MORE AMENITIES
1. Complimentary Wi-Fi
2. Text Line for room requests
3. All rooms are non-smoking
4. In-room safe
5. Mini Fridge
6. Coffeemaker
7. iHome docking station
8. Turndown service is available upon request of housekeeping
9. Free newspaper upon request
10. If you need a microwave, one can be supplied to your room for a small fee

˙ Magic Tip ˙
Depending on your room location, we have noticed slow speeds with Wi-Fi. In the club rooms, we had better access than further outside. Yet another reason to request a closer room to the accommodations.

Staying with Pets
The Hard Rock offers pet stays for additional fees, starting at $50 per night and a maximum of $150 for the stay. If you have a dog that is potty trained and doesn't need a lot of exercise, the Hard Rock could be perfect for your needs. There is a small outdoor area for your pet to relieve itself and even room service treat options for dogs. However, if you have a dog with more exercise needs, this may not be the best choice, as Hard Rock is a bit strict and dogs are expected to stay in the room.

Velvet Sessions
See rock and roll legends in this intimate venue. These events happen about once a month and we recommend getting tickets in advance in case the show sells out. Check out the show schedule:
www.hardrockhotelorlando.com/velvet-sessions.htm

LOEWS PORTOFINO BAY

Best for: Adults, Teens, and Conference Groups
Theme: Italian Resort
Cost: $$$–$$$$
Location: 15-minute walking distance to parks and CityWalk, 10-minute water taxi ride

Review: Portofino Bay has a European charm unlike anywhere else in Orlando. If you are looking for a quieter hotel, Portofino Bay is a great choice. This luxury hotel offers stunning views, delicious dining, and premium rooms. At night, the hotel's waterfront plaza comes to life with a guests strolling to the many dining locations. Though you can walk to the parks and CityWalk, it's just a quick water taxi ride to the entrances. Overall, we enjoy the Portofino Bay for its amenities and proximity to the parks. Though Hard Rock is much closer and has the superior pool, Loews houses some fine eateries, charm, and décor that leave a great impression.

Note: Portofino Bay tends to house conferences throughout the year. At these times, the place can become packed and availability may be low. To avoid this, book as far in advance as possible.

ROOMS & SUITES

The rooms at Portofino Bay have a European feel with the molding accents, clean white bedding, and door styles. The bathrooms are often spacy and the beds are comfortable.

Garden View Room – 450 sq. ft., sleeps up to 5 guests and come with either a king or 2 queen beds. Views are of the green, tropical garden.

Bay View Room – 450 sq. ft., sleeps up to 5 guests. Your room will look out to the to the water. We recommend this room for the best views.

Deluxe Rooms – 490 sq. ft. sleeps up to 3 guests with a king or 2 queens. They also come with a sitting area for lounging and an expansive bathroom.

Deluxe King or 2 Queen Rooms – 490 sq. ft. sleeps up to 5 guests. Our favorite room for the price. These rooms are spacious and have an Italian window that connects to the bathroom. Also available on the club level for extra amenities.

Portofino Parlor Suite with connecting room – Starting at 450 sq. ft. Get a bonus space for a rollaway bed and sleep up to 7. The connecting room can be a King or 2 Queen with bay or garden view. Rollaway beds are $25 per night.

Hospitality Parlor Suite with connecting room – 920 sq. ft. with space up to 5. This suite is designed for entertaining guests and includes sofas, armchairs, kitchenette with fridge and microwave, and two bathrooms with the connecting room. You can attach a King or 2 Queen Garden View room.

Despicable Me Kids' Suites – 650 sq. feet and up to 4 guests. The Minions from *Despicable Me* take over this colorful, kid-friendly room. With specially designed twin beds, curtains, wallpaper and more, this suite attaches to a king room for adults. Additional rollaway or crib upon request with $25/ rollaway bed.

Villa Parlor Suite with connecting room – 1600 sq. ft. and sleeps ten. The largest room with a connecting bay view or garden view suite. There are two separate bedrooms and a large living room area. Rollaway beds are available for $25 per night.

Club – Access to an exclusive area with water, snacks, breakfast bites, beer, wine, and sometimes vodka mixers for adults 21 and older. Unfortunately, the club level guest rooms are pretty far away from the club amenities, so you'll need to walk a bit before getting to the area. The club room is open from 7am to 10pm, daily.

AMENITIES

Pools – Like right out of a Roman aqueduct are blue waters and brick walls. Wade in the water, race down the waterslide, or lounge on the beach chairs. The Hillside Pool is more for adults, offering a calm swimming experience with little noise.

Mandara Spa Fitness Center – Get in a complimentary workout at this hotel's gym. Equipped with treadmills, bicycles, elliptical, weight resistance machines, free weights, a stairmaster, and fitness mats. The room isn't enormous, but it gets the job done for a vacation pump. The fitness center also maps out jogging paths up to 3 miles around the property and houses a locker room with saunas.

Business Center – Print, copy, fax, mail, and e-mail from this all-in-one self-service room. The business center is open 24 hours, 7 days a week, and is very helpful. Some of the items may cost to use, see concierge desk for details.

Mandara Spa – A beautiful and relaxing spa experience. Prepare to spend $150 or more on a massage, though it does offer a set of other services from skincare to body treatments.

Kid's Gifts – For children under 10, Portofino Bay offers a complimentary welcome gift of assorted items for young kids. A "Kids Closet" is also available to borrow with toys, books, a night light, blankets, outlet protectors, and more to make your stay with children more comfortable. Babysitting services are also offered with the concierge. For older kids, board games and an on-site arcade are offered to play.

MORE AMENITIES
1. Complimentary Wi-Fi
2. All rooms are non-smoking
3. In-room safe
4. Mini Fridge
5. Coffeemaker
6. iHome docking station
7. Turndown service is available upon request of housekeeping
8. Free newspaper upon request
9. If you need a microwave, one can be supplied to your room for a small fee
10. Dry Cleaning is available Monday through Saturday, same day, for an additional fee.

Staying with Pets
Portofino Bay offers pet stays for additional fees, starting at $50 per night and a maximum of $150 for the stay. Portofino Bay brags to be one of the better resorts to stay at with pets, as part of Loews hospitality experience. Potty area and walking spots are available around the resort. Still, we recommend a very well potty trained dog that is okay staying in a room for most of the day.

LOEWS ROYAL PACIFIC

Best for: Families, Adults
Theme: Polynesian Resort
Cost: $$$
Location: 10-minute walking distance to parks and CityWalk, 10-minute water taxi ride

Review: Third in line for luxury and proximity to the parks, Royal Pacific feels like a Polynesian paradise centered around a lagoon-style pool. The rooms aren't as pricey as Hard Rock or Portofino Bay, but you get the same benefits including Express Pass Unlimited. Depending on availability, Royal Pacific can be more expensive than Portofino Bay, but this occurrence is quite rare.

ROOMS & SUITES

The rooms at Royal Pacific are undeniably stylish with tropical flares, artwork, and contemporary-style bedding. While these rooms tend to run smaller than the ones at Portofino Bay and Hard Rock, the Kids' room and hospitality parlors are much larger.

Standard – 335 sq. ft., sleeps up to 5 guests and come with either a king or 2 queen beds. Views are of the garden, tropical garden. They also have a desk and chair for office work.

Water View Room – Same as the standard rooms, but with a view of the pool or the water way. We prefer the views of the beautiful water way to watch the boats come and go.

Deluxe Rooms – 490 sq. ft. sleeps up to 3 guests with a king or 2 queens. They also come with a sitting area for lounging and expansive bathroom.

Deluxe King or 2 Queen Rooms – 490 sq. ft. sleeps up to 5 guests. Our favorite room for the price and the deal. These rooms are fairly spacious. Also available on the club level for extra amenities.

Hospitality Parlor Suite with connecting room – 1005 sq. ft. with space up to 5. This suite is designed for entertaining guests and includes sofas, armchairs, kitchenette with fridge and microwave, and two bathrooms with the connecting room. You can attach a King or 2 Queen Garden View room.

Jurassic World Kids' Suites – 670 sq. feet and up to 5 guests. This jungle and dinosaur-themed room brings the fun of *Jurassic World* to a kid-sized space. With specially designed twin beds, curtains, wallpaper and more, this suite attaches to a King bed master bedroom. Additional rollaway or crib upon request with $25/ rollaway bed.

Royal Club – These 335 sq. ft. rooms are either a King or a Queen suite with varying views of the water way, pool, or garden. Access to an exclusive area with water, snacks, breakfast bites, beer, wine, dessert, and sometimes vodka mixers for adults 21 and older. The club room is open from 7am to 9.30pm, daily.

AMENITIES

Pools – This massive and gorgeous pool is surrounded by cabanas, two hot tubs, and even a water play area for kids. Nearly every night there are activities at the pool from hula hoop contests to nightly movies. Cabanas are available for rental at an additional cost, but the rest comes with your reservation.

Mandara Spa – Located in the Loews Portofino Bay Hotel, the location isn't very close, but the spa is relaxing. Prepare to spend $150 or more on a massage, though it does offer a set of other services from skincare to body treatments. The best way to get to Portofino Bay from Royal Pacific is by the free water taxi.

Business Center – Print, copy, fax, mail, and e-mail from this all-in-one self-service room. The business center is open 24 hours, 7 days a week, and is very helpful. Some of the services may have a fee — see concierge desk for details.

Gym – A large 5,000+ sq. ft. exercise room with weights, strength training machines, exercise bikes, stairmaster, ellipticals, a steam room, sauna, and maps to jogging and walking paths up to 3 miles in length.

MORE AMENITIES

1. Complimentary Wi-Fi
2. All rooms are non-smoking
3. In-room safe
4. Mini Fridge
5. Coffeemaker
6. iHome docking station
7. Turndown service is available upon request of housekeeping
8. Free newspaper upon request
9. If you need a microwave, one can be supplied to your room for a small fee
10. Dry Cleaning is available Monday through Saturday, same day, for an additional fee.

Staying with Pets

Royal Pacific offers pet stays for additional fees, starting at $50 per night and a maximum of $150 for the stay. Loews brags to be one of the better resorts to stay at with pets, as part of their hospitality. Potty area and walking spots are available around the resort. Still, we recommend a very well potty trained dog that is okay staying in a room for most of the day.

ENTERTAINMENT

WANTILAN LUAU AT THE WANTILAN PAVILION

See hula dancers and fire spinners while you dine at this buffet show. The luau is usually on Friday nights and the buffet is all-you-can eat and includes sodas, tea, water, wine, beer, and Mai Tais (alcohol for those 21 and older). The Polynesian-inspired food is great and so is the show!

PRICES

Adults: $71 / $81 Priority Seating*
Children 3-9: $36 / $41 Priority Seating*
Children under 3: No cost

Reservations highly recommended
***Note:** Recommended if you want a great view of the stage.*

SHOPPING

Toko Gifts – A small convenience store with snacks, sunscreen, pain killers, toiletries, drinks, and some apparel.

Treasures of Bali – An apparel store with resort-style clothing, swim suits, and even grass skirts. This store also sells Universal Orlando gifts and souvenirs.

LOEWS SAPPHIRE FALLS

Best for: Families, Adults
Theme: Modern and Tropical Resort
Cost: $$$
Location: 10-minute water taxi ride, ½ mile walk to the Parks

Review: A resort hotel with stunning creeks, a large pool, trendy restaurants, and beautiful rooms. Located near Volcano Bay, and between Cabana Bay and Royal Pacific, the hotel aims to please guests looking for an upscale resort hotel without the high cost.

ROOMS & SUITES
These fresh, newly designed rooms are modern, tropical styles. The rooms are even smaller than Royal Pacific, but the design is similar. We like the overall clean layout of these rooms and great for the price.

Standard – 321 sq. ft., sleeps up to 5 guests and come with either a king or 2 queen beds. Views are of the garden, tropical garden. They also have a desk and chair for office work.

Pool View Room – Same as the standard rooms, but with a view of the pool.

Lagoon View Room – Same as the standard rooms, but with a view of the water.

King Suite – 529 sq. ft. sleeps up to 3 guests. They also come with a sitting area for lounging and expansive bathroom.

Hospitality Suite – 1353 sq. ft. with space up to 5. This suite is designed for entertaining guests and includes sofas, kitchenette with fridge and microwave, and a spacious bathroom.

Kids' Suites – 529 sq. feet and up to 5 guests. These attached rooms only allow access to the main hall view the parent room. With specially designed twin beds, curtains, wallpaper and more, it attaches to a king bed master bedroom. Additional rollaway or crib upon request with $25/ rollaway bed.

Sapphire Suite – 851 sq. ft. sleeps up to 5 guests. These large rooms are beautifully designed with a wet bar and large bathrooms. Unfortunately, the room only comes with a king bed, though roll in beds are possible with advanced notice.

AMENITIES

Pools – A large, lagoon-style lagoon is the centerpiece of this resort. There are plenty of lounge chairs, a large hot tub, and even a water slide.

Mandara Spa – Located a bit further aways in the Loews Portofino Bay Hotel. It's worth a trip to this soothing, high-end spa. Prepare to spend $150 or more on a massage, though it does offer a set of other services from skincare to body treatments. The best way to get to Portofino Bay from Sapphire Falls is by water taxi.

Kaline Health and Fitness – A spacious gym with a dry sauna, new weightlifting equipment, ellipticals, treadmills.

MORE AMENITIES
1. Complimentary Wi-Fi
2. All rooms are non-smoking
3. In-room safe
4. Mini Fridge
5. Turndown service is available upon request of housekeeping

Staying with Pets
Royal Pacific offers pet stays for additional fees, starting at $50 per night and a maximum of $150 for the stay. Loews brags to be one of the better resorts to stay at with pets, as part of their hospitality. Potty area and walking spots are available around the resort. Still, we recommend a very well potty trained dog that is okay staying in a room for most of the day.

ENTERTAINMENT

Caribbean Carnaval
An exciting, all-you-can-eat buffet with Caribbean dishes and beer, wine, and cocktail punch included. A 45-minute dance show occurs with live music from 7pm – 7:45pm. If you are staying outside of the resort, parking is free for this dining experience.

PRICES
Adults: $71 / $81 Priority Seating*
Children 3-9: $36 / $41 Priority Seating*
Children under 3: No cost
Reservations highly recommended
*__Note:__ *Recommended if you want a great view of the stage.*

2019 Discount Deal
Kids 9 and under eat free when you book an adult ticket. This deal expires after March 31, 2019. Discount code: KIDSFREEUOR
Booking: **https://www.universalorlando.com/web/en/ us/things-to-do/dining/caribbean-carnaval/index.html**

SHOPPING

The Universal Store – Apparel, accessories, and toys inspired by the characters and attractions at Universal Studios and Islands of Adventure.

CABANA BAY

Best for: Families, Adults
Theme: Swanky Beach Resort
Cost: $$
Location: 15-minute walk or a shuttle

Review: A swanky family-friendly hotel. With the best prices, tons of activities, and a pool with a lazy river, Cabana Bay is often the best choice for families on a budget.

AMENITIES

Pool – A lagoon-style pool with palm trees, lounge chairs, a lazy river for floating, and a waterslide. The second Cabana pool has a beach-like feel with cabanas available for rental.

Free Wi-Fi – Basic internet around the hotel

Jack LaLanne Physical Fitness Studio – A gym with a new weightlifting equipment, ellipticals, treadmills, and classic video fitness instruction by Jack LaLanne.

ROOMS & SUITES

The retro décor is straight out of the 60's. Bright colors, cool designs, and even bright orange chairs add a sense of light fun to Cabana Bay. The hotel is set up perfectly for families of all sizes at an affordable cost with many amenities. Being that this is a family resort, there aren't any rooms with just king beds.

Standard – Sleeps up to 4 guests with 2 queen beds. Views are of the garden, building, or obstructed. They also have a chair and table for crafts.

Poolside Room – Same as the standard rooms, but with a view of the pool.

Volcano Side Room – Same as the standard rooms, but with a view of Volcano Bay.

Courtyard Family Suite – Sleep up to 6 in this larger room with 2 queen beds, large bathroom with his/her sinks, a kitchenette, and a pull-out sofa. These rooms come with various views including poolside and are either in the main building or the tower.

2-Bedroom Suite – A 772-sq ft. room with two baths, three beds, and a pull-out sofa. One room has two full beds and the second smaller room has one queen bed.

Staying with Pets – Pets are not allowed.

ENTERTAINMENT

Galaxy Bowl – A 10-lane bowling alley with an attached restaurant. Cost is $15 per gay for adults and $9 per kid under 12. Games last 60-90 minutes.

Game-O-Rama Arcade – Filled with games from current to old school.

SHOPPING

The Universal Store – Apparel, accessories, and toys inspired by the characters and attractions at Universal Studios and Islands of Adventure

AVENTURA

Best for: Young Adults, Adults
Theme: Modern and Stylish Hotel Tower
Cost: $$
Location: 15-minute walk or a shuttle, 5 minutes to Volcano Bay

Review: Universal's Aventura Hotel is located just steps away from Universal's Volcano Bay water park. The tower-style is modern, sleek, and filled with new technology such as tablets for ordering fresh towels, room service, and even for playing Netflix. The rooms have curved structures and offer sweeping views of the city including the Orlando Eye Ferris Wheel in the distance. The rooftop bar is also set to appeal to young adults. With comfort and style at a great price, Aventura is an upscale getaway for those on a budget.

AMENITIES

Pool – A large, sleek pool at the base of the hotel. It offers a kids splash zone and a fire pit.

Free Wi-Fi – Basic internet around the hotel.

Fitness Center – A gym with a new weightlifting equipment, ellipticals, and treadmills.

Game Room – New arcade games and Virtual Reality!

ROOMS & SUITES

Bright and clean rooms designed to bring some relaxation to your stay. The hotel is smoke-free.

Standard 2 Queen Room – 314 square feet. Sleeps up to 4 guests with 2 queen beds.

Standard King Room – 258 square feet. Sleeps up to 4 guests with 1 king bed.

Deluxe 2 Queen– 385 square feet. Sleeps up to 5 guests with 2 queen beds.

Deluxe King Room – 385 square feet. Sleeps up to 4 guests with 1 king bed.

Skyline View 2 Queen Room – 314 square feet. Sleeps up to 4 guests with 2 queen beds, and has a sweeping view of Orlando or the Universal Resort.

Staying with Pets – Pets are not allowed at this hotel.

SHOPPING

The Universal Store – Apparel, accessories, and toys inspired by the characters and attractions at Universal Studios and Islands of Adventure.

ENDLESS SUMMER

Best for: Families, Young Adults
Theme: Oceanside Rooms and Suites
Cost: $

Review: This upcoming, expansive resort will offer two new hotels: Surfside Inn & Suites and the Dockside Inn & Suites. Surfside is set to open mid-2019 and Dockside will follow in 2020. Surprisingly, these stylish new hotels will be value resorts with nightly costs under $100! For larger families, the suites will stat under $120 per night, making Universal Orlando one of the best value vacation spots in Florida. While these hotels are a bit further from the theme parks, they offer complimentary shuttle transport.

TOP OFF-SITE HOTELS

We've compiled a list of our top choice hotels outside of the Universal Orlando Resort. We still use Orbitz, BookIt.com, or the hotel's website for the best rates.

ROSEN SHINGLE CREEK ORLANDO

Distance from Universal: About 4 miles
Cost: $$ **Star Rating:** 4
Review: Our favorite off-site hotel is the Rosen Shingle Creek. This stunning property is just outside of the Universal Orlando Resort and placed on an award-winning golf course. The staff is friendly, the rooms are beautiful and comfortable, and if you book ahead, you can get a very good deal on a room.
Amenities: Several pools (family, quiet, and kids' wading pool), hot tubs, tennis courts, walking trails, game room, basketball court, volleyball court, fishing (seasonal). Stay at the hotel and receive 25% off of golfing green fees (first round only). Shuttle to Universal is available with reservation: +1 (407) 996-8596
Discounts: The Rosen Shingle Creek offers several theme park vacation packages including tickets to Universal Orlando. For their select packages, visit the hotel's website:
https://www.rosenshinglecreek.com/specials/leisure-packages

THE POINT HOTEL & SUITES

Distance from Universal: About 1.5 miles
Cost: $-$$
Review: A popular hotel for its proximity to the Universal Orlando Resort, the Point Hotel and Suites offer spacious rooms

for a great price. Guests also enjoy the shuttle service to and from the theme parks and airport.

Amenities: Shuttle service to Orlando hotspots (Universal Orlando, Disney, Sea World, and the Orlando International Airport), gym, concierge, business center, Wi-Fi, pool, hot tub

Discounts: Get seasonal discounts and take advantage of promotions for booking early:

https://www.thepointorlando.com/offers.htm

AXIS WEST

Distance from Universal: About 5 miles

Cost: $-$$

Review: These luxury apartments are great for long stays and for families that need more rooms. 1, 2, and 3 bedroom units with kitchens are available at affordable pricing.

Amenities: Units with kitchens (including cookware, microwave, fridge/freezer), washer/dryers in unit, free Wi-Fi, jogging trail, pool, barbecues, gym, pet-friendly

Discounts: Get seasonal discounts and take advantage of promotions for booking early:

https://www.thepointorlando.com/offers.htm

MORE OFF-SITE HOTELS

Hyatt Regency Grand Cypress
1 Grand Cypress Blvd, Orlando, FL 32836
(407) 239-1234 / www.hyatt.com

Star Rating	Our Rating	Price	Shuttle to Universal	Pool
4	A	Deluxe	Yes	Yes

Pros: Beautiful property and rooms. Scheduled shuttle service to and from Universal and Disney theme parks, on-site spa, nearby golfing, rock climbing, and 24-hour fitness center. Pet accommodations available.

Cons: Can be expensive and have a very high resort fee (about $40/night). About a 15-minute drive to the Universal Orlando Resort.

Doubletree by Hilton at the Entrance to Universal Orlando

14200 Bonnet Creek Resort Ln, Orlando, FL 32821
(407) 597-5500 / doubletree3.hilton.com/en/index.html

Star Rating	Our Rating	Price	Shuttle to Universal	Pool
5	A+	Luxury	Yes	Yes

Pros: An affordable 4-star hotel property very close Universal (less than a 5-minute drive). Hilton Honors members can get discounts on rooms and earn points.
Cons: Rooms are a bit dated. Shuttle service to other theme parks must be scheduled 24 hours in advance.

Gaylord Palms Resort

6000 W. Osceola Parkway, Orlando, FL 32821
(407) 586-0000 / www.gaylordpalms.com

Star Rating	Our Rating	Price	Shuttle to Universal	Pool
5	A-	Luxury	Paid	Yes

Pros: Beautiful and affordable 4-star hotel property and rooms. Unique theming including an indoor restaurant on a boat. Shuttle service to Disney theme parks, on-site spa, pools with waterslides, wave pool, on-site alligators, nearby golfing, and 24-hour fitness center. Marriott Rewards members can get discounts on rooms and earn points. 10-minute drive to Epcot.
Cons: Shuttles to Universal are $21/person roundtrip (thus, we recommend taking Lyft). Parking is expensive and can become backed up on busy weekends and holidays. The hotel is about a 25-minute drive to Universal Orlando.

Ritz-Carlton Grande Lakes

4012 Central Florida Pkwy, Orlando, FL 32837
(407) 206-2400 / www.ritzcarlton.com

Star Rating	Our Rating	Price	Shuttle to Universal	Pool
5	A	Luxury	Yes	Yes

Pros: Elegant 5-star hotel property and stunning rooms. Shuttle service to and from Universal Orlando, Disney theme parks, and SeaWorld. On-site spa, butterfly garden, kids play area, bocce ball courts, 18-hole golfing, and fitness center. Superior service.

Cons: Expensive, so if you're looking for a bargain on a 5-star resort, you may want to try the Waldorf Astoria (though we prefer the Ritz Carlton or the Four Seasons). About 20 to 25-minute drive to the Magic Kingdom, Epcot, or Universal Orlando.

CHAPTER NINE

UNIVERSAL CITYWALK

INTRODUCTION

The Universal CityWalk is a mall meets entertainment hotspot. Guests do not need paid admission to enter Universal CityWalk. During the day its home to a collection of shops from Fossil to Fresh Produce, as well as chain restaurants like Bubba Gump and the Hard Rock Cafe. At night, CityWalk's dance clubs light up and locals pour into the area. You can also catch a movie, sing karaoke, or see the Blue Man Group perform.

We love the scenery in CityWalk with its neon lights, elaborately themed restaurants, and the surprising nightlife. Unfortunately, the food in CityWalk is hit or miss. A delicious looking burger on a menu might be $14 and bland. While the colorful yet unassuming Mexican restaurant is a delicious! Our reviews are honest and fairly straight forward so that you can be guided toward the winners and keep away from the duds.

ENTERTAINMENT

BLUE MAN GROUP

This alien-like stage show mixes weird music performance. If psychedelic alien raves are your scene, the don't miss the Blue Man group. Tickets start at $60.

Discount tickets are sometimes available if you bundle with theme park tickets on UniversalOrlando.com or visit:

www.blueman.com/orlando/special-offers

AMC UNIVERSAL CINEPLEX 20 WITH IMAX

See a newly released movie or experience the stunning visuals of IMAX in this 20 screen movie theater. The theater is a tad bit dated, but the quality screens and sound make up for the lack of style.

CITYWALK'S RISING STAR

Take karaoke to the next level with a live band and even backup singers. The audience area is intimate and the show is fun to cheer on the performers. Mostly drinks with a few choice beverages. Open daily from 8PM–2AM.

⋆ **Magic Tip** ⋆

If you'd like to perform, get there and choose your song by 9pm to get called on stage.

HARD ROCK LIVE

See big name music stars, comedians, and DJs in this colosseum that fits up to 3,000 concerts-goers.

For event calendar and tickets:

www.hardrock.com/live/locations/orlando/calendar.aspx

HOLLYWOOD DRIVE-IN GOLF

Play miniature golf in the horror or sci-fi movies! This colorful and creative course has fun for all ages. Choose from The Haunting of Ghostly Greens or Invaders from Planet Putt Open from 9AM – 2AM. For discount tickets, book in advance:

www.hollywooddriveingolf.com

NIGHT CLUBS

RED COCONUT CLUB

A night club and lounge for those 21 and older. The tropical, Miami feel mixes socializing with live DJ music. Drinks are moderately priced. Open from 8PM – 2AM.

THE GROOVE

A night club and lounge for those 21 and older. A spacious dance floor with a live DJ. Drinks are moderately priced. This place gets packed on the weekends, so get there before 10PM if you want to avoid a line.

SHOPS

Element – Skateboarding clothes and accessories

Fossil – Leather clothes and accessories

Fresh Produce – Women's fashionable and brightly colored clothing

Hart and Huntington Tattoo Company – An authentic tattoo parlor. Must be 18 or older.

P!Q – Unique gifts and "designer toys"

Quiet Flight Surf Shop – Beach clothing and accessories

The Island Clothing Store – Casual wear from Tommy Bahama and other island designers

Universal Studios Store – Clothing and gifts inspired by Universal Studios. Get everything from Marvel to Harry Potter in this unique shop.

CHAPTER TEN

DINING

INTRODUCTION

As we've said before, the food at Universal Orlando isn't nearly as thrilling as the rides—though there are exceptions. For those of you looking for more than a bland burger or a slapped-together sandwich, this chapter is for you. We've searched the resort from top to bottom to find the best eats around (we also know which ones to avoid). The best gems aren't always the most expensive or the most obvious. Some of these better dining locations deserve a spot on your to-do list. In this chapter, we venture through the Universal Orlando eaters—from the theme park to the hotels and the fun of CityWalk—and help you plan where to dine.

DINING TYPES

Bars and Lounges – Areas with open seating and typically a full bar.

Quick Service – Fast order meals where you often choose your own seating.

Table Service – Restaurants with a waiter. It is suggested you that you tip based on the service you receive.

UNIVERSAL DINING PLAN

Universal Orlando offers special dining packages for use around the resort. The Universal Dining Plan (UDP) is designed for guests to pre-pay for the food that they plan to enjoy during their vacation. While Universal touts its dining plan as a way to save money, for many guests this simply isn't the case. So, think of UDP as more of an "all-inclusive" cost rather than a way to pinch pennies. However, we've discovered that UDP *can* save you a load of cash or end up costing you more, depending on how well you plan before your visit. Overall, we think that UDP can be great option for visiting guests, and with our tips, you can make the most of this program. UDP can be redeemed at over a 100 dining spots around Universal Orlando that take part of this program. These include the theme parks and CityWalk (we note most of their locations later in this chapter).

QUALIFICATIONS

To buy one of the Universal Dining Plans, you'll need to pre-purchase a vacation or ticket package through UniversalOrlando.com or over the phone. The Coca-Cola "freestyle" Souvenir Cup can be purchased on your visit date as a refillable drink mug.

Note: *The "freestyle" Souvenir Cup and Universal Quick Service dining plans can also be purchased during Halloween Horror Nights.*

DINING PLAN TYPES

UNIVERSAL DINING PLAN

Cost: $63.89/Adult and $24.48/Child (ages 3-9) per day

Credits per guest, per day:

- 1 Table Service Meal (*includes 1 entree, 1 dessert, and 1 non-alcoholic beverage per day*)
- 1 Quick Service Meal (*includes 1 entree and 1 non-alcoholic beverage per day*)
- 1 Snack
- 1 Non-Alcoholic Beverage

UNIVERSAL DINING PLAN – QUICK SERVICE
Cost: $25.55/Adult and $17.03/Child (ages 3-9) per day
Credits per guest, per day:
- 1 Quick Service Meal
- 1 Snack
- 1 Non-Alcoholic Beverage

UNIVERSAL DINING PLAN – QUICK SERVICE + SOUVENIR CUP
Cost: $31.94/Adult and $23.42/Child (ages 3-9)
Credits per guest, per day:
- 1 Quick Service Meal
- 1 Snack
- 1-Day Unlimited Coca-Cola "Freestyle" Beverage

COCA-COLA "freestyle" SOUVENIR CUP
Cost: $15.99 / day (plus tax)
- 1-Day Unlimited Coca-Cola "Freestyle" Beverage

⋆ **Magic Tip** ⋆
Get 10% off the total of your Universal Dining Plan Quick Service purchase by using your American Express card!

DINING PLAN TIPS

If you're a heavy soda drinker (or are planning on having about 3 or more per day), the Souvenir Cup is a great value, especially when combined with the Quick Service dining plan. You can also save money if you're willing to try the most expensive items on the menu. For example, a steak dinner would normally cost more than a hamburger, so it's a better value to select the steak.

Snacks can be used for more cart items including popcorn, ice cream, and, yes, Butterbeer in the Wizarding World of Harry Potter! Butterbeer is one of the more expensive snacks around Universal, so we recommend using your credit for that.

Keep in mind that while the UDP works at the Harry Potter Quick Service locations, character dining experiences (like Marvel and Despicable Me) are not included, even as a Table Service credit. Currently, none of the hotels take part of Universal Dining Plan either. Finally, gratuity isn't included with the UDP, so make sure you bring cash with you to tip (Table Service restaurants only).

As we've said before, depending on your needs, the Universal Disney Plan may not save you money. It may even cost you more than just paying out of pocket for your meals. If you're not interested in planning all of your dining before you head to the parks, we don't recommend the UDP. It might feel overwhelming to pre-plan your vacation, meal by meal for each day. However, the Quick Service plan may work better for your needs in this occasion. It almost always works out to a wash or a slight savings. With this plan, you can grab food when you're hungry and not worry about getting the best bang for your buck.

Also, children ten and older with smaller appetites may end up costing you more than they'll eat. While some ten-year-olds eat as much as an adult, many do not. Nonetheless, you'll pay the same for a ten-year-old boy as you would an adult man. Furthermore, children who are picky and inconsistent eaters may not benefit from UDP. Make sure you review kids' menus before booking.

RESTAURANTS WITH UNIVERSAL DINING PLAN
We've marked all of the restaurants offering the Universal Dining Plan with "**Ω**"

OUR RESTAURANT PRICING
$ – Under $10 (typically snack carts)
$$ – $10 - $15 (typically Quick Service Restaurants)
$$$ – $15 - $30 (Table Service Restaurants)
$$$$ – More than $30 (Fine Dining)

LOOK FOR THE HEARTS
We also list our favorites from snacks to dining locations. Just look for the "**♥**" next to the item to see our most recommended!

CAFE LA BAMBA
Hollywood
Description: Meet some of your favorite characters including the Minions from *Despicable Me* while dining on American favorites.
Type: Character Dining Cafeteria
Price: $$
Menu Items: BBQ ribs, steak, roasted chicken, salad, burritos, tacos
Recommendation: Chipotle BBQ Ribs or Chimichurri Skirt Steak

MEL'S DRIVE-IN Ω
Hollywood
Description: A classic 50's diner styled after its Hollywood, CA location. Great theming, but the bland menu could use a revamp.
Type: Quick service
Price: $$
Menu Items: burgers, onion rings, French fries, root beer floats, and shakes
Recommendation: The burgers are okay, but the onion rings are a good choice as a side

FAST FOOD BOULEVARD Ω ♥
Springfield
Description: A collection of cafeteria dining spots styled after locations and characters from The Simpsons.
Type: Quick Service
Price: $-$$
Dining Choices:
Cletus' Chicken Shack – fried chicken and milkshakes
Frying Dutchman – fried seafood and milkshakes
Krusty Burger – burgers and shakes
Lisa's Teahouse of Horror – vegetarian options and mixed tea drinks
Luigi's Pizza – pizzas and milkshakes

Recommendation: Chicken and Waffle sandwich (Cletus' Chicken Shack), Basket of Calamari (Frying Dutchman), or a Krusty Burger (Krusty Burger)

FINNEGAN'S BAR & GRILL Ω
New York

Description: An Irish-American pub. The options here are hit or miss, but the environment is fun. Finnegan's looks like a place on a move set. The food is also very similar to what is served in the Harry Potter restaurants.

Type: Table Service

Price: $$$

Menu Items: Cornish pasti, potato and onion webb, scotch eggs, chicken fingers, bangers and mash, shepherd's pie, fish, chicken, sandwiches, burgers, Guinness Beef Stew

Recommendation: Cornish pasti or fish and chips

THE LEAKY CAULDRON Ω ♥
Diagon Alley

Description: Dine like a witch or wizard in this stunningly detailed British restaurant. See artifacts straight from the *Harry Potter* series and savor delicious offerings inspired by the movies and books! The Leaky Cauldron is a one of our favorite dining spots in Universal.

Type: Quick Service

Price: $$

Menu Items: fish and chips, bangers and mash, Guinness stew, fisherman's pie, toad in the hole, mini pies, chicken sandwich, *Harry Potter*-themed desserts, Butterbeer

Recommendation: Specialty Chicken Sandwich ♥, Fish & Chips, Butterbeer potted cream ♥

⋆ **Magic Tip** ⋆

If you're deciding between The Leaky Cauldron and the Three Broomsticks in Hogsmeade, we enjoy the food better at The Three Broomsticks.

LOMBARD'S SEAFOOD GRILLE Ω
San Francisco

Description: San Franciscan seafood diner on the water. With its rustic charm and view of the Universal waterway, you'll feel like you've been transported to an authentic Californian restaurant on the wharf!

Type: Table Service

Price: $$$

Menu Items: shrimp, fried calamari, clam chowder, salads, fish, pasta, burgers, sandwiches

Recommendation: Crab cake sandwich, shrimp mac and cheese, lobster roll

LOUIE'S ITALIAN RESTAURANT Ω ♥
New York

Description: Grab pizza by the slice or a sub at this cafeteria-style eatery. The ambiance is lackluster (feels like a dingy cafeteria), but pizza is pretty good!

Type: Quick Service

Price: $-$$

Menu Items: pizzas, subs, chicken parmesan, pasta, Caesar salad

Recommendation: Jumbo pizza slice (any flavor) ♥

RICHTER'S BURGER CO. Ω
San Francisco

Description: Chow down on a burger of your choice in this swanky, wharf-themed cafeteria. We wish the burgers were better, but they're not terrible. Still, we'd recommend heading to the Hard Rock Café in CityWalk for a burger instead.

Type: Quick Service

Price: $-$$

Menu Items: burgers, chicken sandwiches, salads, fries, cheese fries, soda floats, shakes

Recommendation: Frisco Shake (chocolate or vanilla)

UNIVERSAL STUDIOS' CLASSIC MONSTER CAFE Ω
New York

Description: American classics with monster-themed meals. Inside, walk through classic sets like Mockingbird Lane from The Munsters.

Type: Quick Service
Price: $-$$
Menu Items: burgers, pizza, ribs, chicken, turkey leg, salad, fries, mac and cheese
Recommendation: Pizza ♥ or Chicken and Rib Platter

MORE EATS

Beverly Hills Boulangerie ($-$$) Ω – Located in Hollywood. Try a sweet, latte, or sandwich in this Beverly Hills-themed quick service eatery.

Ben and Jerry's Ice Cream ($) – Located in New York. Some very delicious ice cream from the famous brand.

Bumblebee Man's Taco Truck ($) – Located in Springfield. Try one of Bumblebee Man's crafted tacos, they come 2 per order right out of a taco truck. We recommend the juicy Korean Beef Taco for a delicious Asian-Mexican fusion.

Chez Alcatraz ($) – Located in San Francisco. Bar food and drinks in a hut by the wharf. The bartenders are usually fast pourers and attentive. However, on busy days, there likely won't be room to sit around this small area.

Duff Brewery ($) – Located in Springfield. Try a draft beer (ages 21 and older) in an outdoor brewing area inspired by *The Simpsons*.

Flaming Moe's ($) – Located in Springfield. Try draft beer (ages 21 and older) or a Flaming Moe ♥ (non-alcoholic) that fizzes as you drink it! The decor in Flaming Moe's looks just like in The Simpsons. You can even have a drink with Barney Grumble!

Florean Fortescue's Ice-Cream Parlour ($) – Located in Diagon Alley. Harry Potter-themed ice cream served in a waffle cone, cup, or souvenir glass. We recommend the Butterbeer soft serve or sticky toffee pudding!

Fountain of Fair Fortune ($) ♥– Located in Diagon Alley. Harry Potter-themed eats and drinks. Try the minty Fishy Green Ale!

The Hopping Pot ($) ♥– Located in Diagon Alley. Harry Potter-themed eats and drinks. Try the Butterbeer here. They also have a fine selection of alcoholic beers for those 21 and older. Try taking a sip of both Butter Beer and a draft beer at the same time— we love it!

Lard Lads ($) ♥– Located in Springfield. Donuts and more donuts! Try the Big Pink, an enormous donut with enough sweetness to feed a family!
· **Magic Tip** ·
If Lard Lads runs out of donuts or has too long of a line, visit the Kwik-E-Mart in Springfield and buy one there.

San Francisco Pastry Company ($-$$) Ω – Located in San Francisco. Daily baked breads to make sandwiches and baked goods. We recommend trying one of their tasty muffins.

Starbucks Coffee ($) – Located in New York. The world-famous brewing company brings its brand to Universal. Get your favorite drinks here.

ISLANDS OF ADVENTURE

BLONDIE'S Ω
Toon Lagoon
Description: Sandwiches made big enough to feed Dagwood from the Blondie comic strips. Similar to subway, you can style your own sub.
Type: Quick Service
Price: $$
Menu Items: sandwiches, hot dogs, potato salad
Recommendation: Dagwood Sandwich

THE BURGER DIGS Ω
Jurassic Park
Description: Serving up burgers and fries in this *Jurassic Park*-themed cafeteria. When choosing dining in Jurassic Park, we prefer Thunder Falls Terrace over Burger Digs as we find the food and ambiance better.
Type: Quick Service
Price: $$
Menu Items: Burgers, fries, onion rings
Recommendation: Onion Rings

CAFE 4 Ω
Marvel Super Hero Island
Description: A pizza cafeteria styled after Marvel Comics' Fantastic 4. The inside looks a 90's comic café, and the pizza is fairly good.
Type: Quick Service
Price: $$
Menu Items: pizza, Caesar salad, pasta, sandwiches
Recommendation: Pizza with your choice of toppings

CAPTAIN AMERICA DINER Ω
Marvel Super Hero Island
Description: A burger cafeteria styled after Marvel Comics' Captain America. The inside looks a 90's comic café, and the burgers are just okay.
Type: Quick Service
Price: $$
Menu Items: burgers, salad, onion rings, fries, sandwiches, shakes
Recommendation: Onion rings

CIRCUS MCGURKUS CAFE STOO-PENDOUS Ω ♥
Seuss Landing
Description: A brightly colored and well-themed diner in a Seuss-style circus tent! See your favorite Dr. Seuss characters as you dine on American favorites.
Type: Quick Service
Price: $$
Menu Items: pasta, fried chicken, burgers, salad, sandwiches, pizza, Dippin' Dots ice cream

Recommendation: Fried Chicken Platter (comes in 2-piece and 3-piece) ♥

COMIC STRIP CAFE Ω
Toon Lagoon
Description: A burger and hot dog cafeteria with comic book decor. The food is just okay.
Type: Quick Service
Price: $$
Menu Items: burgers, hot dogs, salad, onion rings, fish, sandwiches, shakes
Recommendation: Fish and chips, onion rings

CONFISCO GRILLE Ω ♥
Port of Entry
Description: Taste around the world with this hodgepodge of selections. Even the restaurant's décor amplifies a medley of cultures from around the world. From Italian and Mexican to Asian and American, there's something at Confisco for everyone. The food here is pretty good, and even better if you know what to order (see our recommendations).
Type: Table Service
Price: $$$
Menu Items: spinach and artichoke dip, hummus, nachos, fried calamari, wings, salads, pizzas, fish, pad thai, fajitas, pasta, curry chicken, sandwiches, burgers, wraps
Recommendation: Chef's Signature Oven Fire Pizza ♥, An Adventure in Fajitas, Our House Specialty Pad Thai

DOC SUGRUE'S KEBAB HOUSE Ω ♥
The Lost Continent
Description: Try a flavorful kebab and other Mediterranean cuisine at this delicious window-service eatery.
Type: Quick Service
Price: $$
Menu Items: chicken, beef, and vegetarian kebab skewers, Greek salad, hummus

Recommendation: All of the kebabs are very tasty ♥. The meat and vegetables are marinated and come with pita bread and Greek Yogurt dipping sauce.

FIRE EATER'S GRILL Ω
The Lost Continent

Description: American and Greek favorites from a window-service eatery. Eat here if you're craving a chili cheese dog (though they aren't very flavorful), otherwise head to Doc Sugrue's in the Lost Continent as the food is better.

Type: Quick Service

Price: $-$$

Menu Items: chicken fingers, chili cheese dog, gyro, salads, chili cheese fries

Recommendation: Chicken fingers

MYTHOS RESTAURANT Ω
The Lost Continent

Description: A wonderfully themed Mediterranean restaurant with mediocre food. If only the cascading waterfalls and the perfectly detailed architecture were enough! Mythos is known for its beauty and stale pita bread. Even the salads are mostly iceberg lettuce. While the food is certainly edible, it's a big letdown. If you're dying to eat here, play it safe with flatbread or a burger.

Type: Table Service

Price: $$$

Menu Items: flat bread, fried calamari, salad, pad thai, risotto, fish, Italian pasta, sandwiches, burger

Recommendation: Spanakopita dip, a flatbread, Mythos Signature Burger

⋆ **Magic Tips** ⋆

Mythos is the most popular dining destination in the theme parks, so get a reservation before you go. Even on not-so-busy days, we've seen people wait hours to dine here.

PIZZA PREDATTORIA Ω
Jurassic Park

Description: Grab a slice of pizza in this outdoor picnic area. The pizza is pretty good.

Type: Quick Service

Price: $$
Menu Items: pizza, meatball subs, salads
Recommendation: Meat Lovers Pizza

THE THREE BROOMSTICKS Ω ♥

Hogsmeade

Description: Our favorite dining spot in the Universal Orlando Resort! The *Harry Potter* homages in this restaurant are magical and the food is very tasty. There's often a short line before ordering, which can be handy for indecisive diners. The food is on display in windows for you to see how it's prepared. Once you order, you'll wait for your tray and then the dining staff will find you a table. This way, you always know that you're sitting somewhere with enough seats and that's been properly cleaned before you dine!

Type: Quick Service

Price: $$

Menu Items: fish and chips, Cornish pasties, spare ribs, chicken, turkey leg, salads, shepherd's pie, Butterbeer, *Harry Potter*-themed desserts

Recommendation: We've enjoyed every item on this menu, but our favorites include the chicken and ribs platter ♥, fish & chips, and cornish pasties (they are sort of like empanadas). For dessert, try the Butterbeer potted cream ♥ (a pudding-like delicious dessert flavored like Butterbeer)

* **Magic Tips** *

If you're planning on lunch at the Three Broomsticks on a busy day, we recommend getting there by 11:30am to avoid the lunch rush. For later lunching, head there after 2:30pm. Dinner at The Three Broomsticks isn't as popular as midday dining.

THUNDER FALLS TERRACE Ω ♥

Jurassic Park

Description: One of the better-themed cafeteria dining experiences, Thunder Falls Terrace is styled after the visitor areas of Jurassic Park. Get savory BBQ and American favorites.

Type: Quick Service

Price: $$

Menu Items: BBQ ribs, chicken, wraps, burgers, salads, soups

Recommendation: Chicken & Ribs ♥

WIMPY'S Ω
Toon Lagoon
Description: Burgers and fries served counter style. You can get a combination meal served with a slice of apple pie.
Type: Quick Service
Price: $$
Menu Items: burgers, fries, onion rings, apple pie
Recommendation: Apple pie

MORE EATS

Backwater Bar ($-$$) ♥– Located in Port of Entry. A full service "dive bar" (it's not actually a dive, but made to look like one) serving up tasty specialty cocktails and wine for those 21 and older. This is one of our favorite spots when traveling with adults!

Cinnabon ($) – Located in Port of Entry. A chain bakery serving up their famously delicious cinnamon rolls.

Croissant Moon Bakery ($) Ω – Located in Port of Entry. A great place to grab a muffin for breakfast. However, if not fresh, their food items can be pretty bland.

Green Eggs and Ham ($) Ω – Located in Seuss Landing. A seasonal offering of—what else—green eggs and ham. This shop isn't usually open, but if it is, you should try the famous offering!

Hog's Head pub ($-$$) ♥ – Located in Hogsmeade. Try Butterbeer or a Harry Potter mixed drink or beer (for those 21 and older). The decor is very cool in here with the moving hog's head placed on the wall. We recommend the Pear Dazzle, a vodka-based mixed drink with a lightly sweet flavor. For the kids, have them try a Pumpkin Juice out of the bottle or Butterbeer.

Hop On Pop Ice Cream Shop ($) – Located in Seuss Landing. Frozen treats styled after Dr. Seuss' books. Try a Brownie Sundae in a Waffle Bowl.

Moose Juice, Goose Juice ($) – Located in Seuss Landing. Snacks and drinks inspired by the imaginative creatures by Dr. Seuss. Try their Goose Juice (a frozen sour green apple blended beverage).

Starbucks Coffee ($) – Located in Port of Entry. The world-famous coffee company brings its brand to Islands of Adventure. Get your favorite drinks here.

The Watering Hole ($-$$) – Located in Jurassic Park. Those 21 and older can grab a draft beer or mixed drink here. They also serve nachos and pretzels, but the food often tastes stale.

VOLCANO BAY

Bambu ($-$$) Ω – Burgers, hot dogs, chicken tenders, and salads. We recommend trying the Pretzel Dog. The pineapple upside down cake is very good, too.

Dancing Dragons Boat Bar ($) – Spot this bar by looking for the sails printed with floral designs. A perfect place to grab an island-inspired mixed drink (for those 21 and older).

The Feasting Frog ($-$$) Ω – A frog-shaped hut serving tacos and poke bowls. The plantain chips and guacamole are a delicious surprise!

Kunuku Boat Bar ($) – Fruit-infused specialty drinks and beers (for those 21 and older). The drinks can be a bit sugary.

Kohola Reef Restaurant & Social Club ($$) Ω ♥ – Grab lunch at this oasis-style restaurant. The Mango BBQ Pulled Pork Sandwich packs some great flavor.

Whakawaiwai Eats ($-$$) Ω ♥ – Quick service flatbreads that are delicious! We recommend stopping by here for a bite.

CITYWALK

ANTOJITOS AUTHENTIC MEXICAN FOOD Ω / ♥

Description: A delicious Mexican dining experience with live music

Type: Table service

Open: Dinner

Price: $$ – $$$

Review: Antojitos is certainly one of the better restaurants in Universal Orlando. We love the south-of-the-border ambiance with colorful décor, friendly staff, and mariachi music playing around the restaurant. We're perhaps a bit snobbish when it comes to Mexican food, and their menu choices are very, very good! In the evenings, especially on weekends, live musicians hit the stage to perform. If you're just stopping in for a drink, they have an extensive tequila selection. During the week, you likely won't need a reservation, but weekends and holidays, we recommend one. Call (407) 224-3663 to reserve.

Menu Items: Mexican-style foods—chips and guacamole, nachos, beans, quesadillas, taco salad, enchiladas, fajitas, tacos, carnitas, burritos, chimichangas, tortilla soup, margaritas, tequila, cocktails, soda

For Kids: Tacos, quesadillas, empanadas, grilled chicken breast

Recommendations: Chimichanga (fried burrito stuffed with marinated chicken, cheese, salsa, guacamole, and served with black beans and rice)

Fajitas (choose from chicken, vegetable, carne, or a combination of two. Freshly grilled on a skillet and served with warm, house made tortillas, guacamole, sour cream, cheese, and pico de gallo).

Adults (21 and older): Try any of their margaritas

BOB MARLEY A TRIBUTE TO FREEDOM Ω

Description: Jamaican dining with live reggae styled after Bob Marley

Type: Table service and Dance bar

Open: Dinner and Late Night

Price: $$

Review: Eat, drink, and dance the night away to live reggae in this unique setting. The food isn't remarkable, so we recommending visiting for the small club scene. Bob Marley's has an event nearly every night of the week. The dinner menu is famous for "belly full" items that make you feel stuffed.

Menu Items: Jamaican jerk chicken, salad, lamb skewers, oxtail stew, curry chicken, fish, sodas, full bar

For Kids: Mac and cheese, chicken tenders, burger with rice

Recommendation: Reggae Jamaican Jerk Chicken

Adults (21 and older): Caribbean Calamity – Bacardi rum and banana liqueur with orange and pineapple juices

BUBBA GUMP SHRIMP CO. ♥

Type: Table service

Description: *Forest Gump*-themed dining with plenty of shrimp and American favorites

Open: Lunch and Dinner

Price: $$

Review: The restaurant from *Forest Gump* comes to life with some very delicious food! Bubba Gump's has fun waiters, themed rooms from the movie, and unforgettable food. If you're a fan of fried shrimp, we highly recommend this place. However, the fried chicken is especially good, too. Before you order, your waiter asks *Forest Gump* trivia—it's a lot of fun, even if you haven't seen the movie in years. As far as chain restaurants go, Bubba Gump wins the prize for overall customer satisfaction from us.

Menu Items: Burger, shrimp, salad, clam chowder, sandwiches, fried chicken, cocktails, beer, wine, soda

Kids: hamburger, hot dog, chicken fingers

Recommendation: Shrimpers Heaven ♥ – breaded coconut shrimp, chilly shrimp, fried shrimp, and tempura shrimp served with fries and dipping sauce. It's a lot of food, but shrimp lovers will be in heaven.

Mama's Southern Fried Chicken – tastes like a homemade southern boneless chicken meal. Served with mashed potatoes, gravy, and corn.

Adult (21 and older): Lava Flow – a sweet mix of rum, coconut cream, strawberries, banana, and pineapple juice. The glass is large and tastes like a smoothie with rum.

THE COWFISH Ω ♥

Description: A clever name! The Cow stands for burgers and the Fish stands for sushi. Grab either at this trendy dining joint.

Type: Table service

Open: Lunch and Dinner

Price: $$–$$$

Review: Cowfish is sort of genius because there's something for everyone. The sushi lovers will get their fill and those just craving a great burger will feel satisfied. This multi-level building is known for its decent sized portions and crafty menu options. We love sushi and burgers, but their signature dish, Burgushi—where they mix sushi and hamburgers—sounded strange at first. However, the rolls were extremely delicious and a must try. Even if you don't like sushi, the Burgushi's taste will appeal to most hamburger fans (and, don't worry, they skip the seaweed).

Menu Items: Sushi, burgers, salads, calamari, edamame, sandwiches, cocktails, wine, beer, shakes, soda, desserts

For Kids: Chicken nuggets, grilled cheese, PB&J, mac and cheese, mini burgers, sushi

Recommendation:

The All-American Bacon Double Cheeseburgooshi ♥

HARD ROCK CAFE ORLANDO

Type: Table service

Description: An American restaurant with rock n roll memorabilia

Open: Breakfast, Lunch, and Dinner

Price: $$

Review: The world-famous restaurant chain finds its Colosseum-shaped home in Orlando. We love the Hard Rock Cafe's exterior with weathered, Roman amphitheater structure. There's a sort of fun, larger-than-life Vegas feel to this multi-level diner. Like most other Hard Rock Cafes, the food is mostly burgers, sodas, and alcohol. Still, the restaurants serves one of the better burgers at the Universal Orlando Resort.

Menu Items:

Breakfast: eggs, bacon, omelet, chicken and waffles, French toast, waffle, mimosas, bloody mary, coffee, soda

Lunch and Dinner: burgers, sandwiches, salad, nacho, wings, potato skins, barbecue, shakes, desserts, cocktails, beer, wine, soda

Kids: hamburger, hot dog, chicken tenders, fish sticks, mac and cheese, cheese pizza, pasta, chicken breast, root beer float

Recommendation:
Breakfast: Chicken and Waffles
Lunch and Dinner: Hickory Barbecue Bacon Cheeseburger
Dessert: Hot Fudge Brownie, served with Ben and Jerry's vanilla ice cream with melted hot fudge. The apple cobbler is pretty good, too!

JIMMY BUFFET'S MARGARITAVILLE Ω

Description: An island themed dining experience with nightly live music

Type: Table service

Open: Lunch, Dinner and Late Night

Price: $$

Review: Margaritaville brings nightly live music, great drinks, and tasty offerings to CityWalk. The live music is great with rock and pop covers, and the bar has friendly staff. The food is pretty good, too. Nothing fancy, just a good time with burgers, fries, seafood, and plenty to drink. Kids also like Margaritaville because of the lively atmosphere.

Menu Items: Burgers, salads, sandwiches, tacos, shrimp, fish, fried chicken, steak, seafood mac and cheese, chicken breast, vegetarian, beer, wine, cocktails, margaritas
Kids: Burger, fish and chips, fried shrimp, chicken strips, pasta, mac and cheese

Recommendation: Fish Tacos, Crispy Coconut Shrimp, or Cheeseburger in Paradise
Adults (21 and older): Who's to Blame Margarita

· Magic Tip ·
There are two bars at Margaritaville. The inside one can get a bit packed, so if you're just looking for a margarita, try the outdoor one. Both are excellent choices for drinks.
For a schedule of bands, visit:
www.margaritavilleorlando.com

PAT O'BRIEN'S ORLANDO Ω

Description: A dueling piano Cajun restaurant and bar

Type: Table service

Open: Dinner and Late Night Music Bar

Price: $$ $$$

Review: Step onto Bourbon Street at this brick house filled with dueling pianos, a full bar, and even a water fountain with fire! If you're into the dueling piano scene, where two piano players face off in song, Pat O'Brien's is your place. The food is nothing to write home about, but they pour strong drinks! The bar is open late, 2am, nightly. If you visit after 9pm, you may have to pay a cover fee.

Menu Items: Steak, pasta, fish, salad, gumbo, jambalaya, crawfish, burger, andouille sausage, chicken, mint julep, beer, wine, mixed drinks

Kids: hamburger, hot dog, chicken fingers

Recommendation: We haven't loved anything here, but the O'Brien's Burger and N' Awlin's Po-Boy are decent

NBC SPORTS GRILL Ω

Type: Table service

Description: A New American restaurant with sports TV

Open: Lunch, Dinner and Late Night (1:30am)

Price: $$–$$$

Review: The flashy, large televisions on the outside of the NBC Sports Grill are certainly eye catching. Even if you don't like sports, you'll likely want to check out the commotion. However, NBC Sports Grill is strictly for the sport fans. The food is pretty good and the inside just looks like a chain restaurant with televisions.

Menu Items: Sliders, burgers, fried calamari, poutine, nachos, wings, lettuce wraps, salad, steak, sandwich, fish tacos, pasta, desserts, beer, full bar, cocktails, wine, soda

Kids: hamburger, hot dog, chicken tenders, fish sticks, mac and cheese, cheese pizza, pasta, chicken breast, root beer float

Recommendation:

Appetizer: Wisconsin Cheese Curds – fried cheddar and spicy tomato jam

Entrees: Wisconsin Burger – It's all in the cheese! Cheddar, thick bacon, lettuce, tomato, and a brioche bun. Also comes with your choice of fries or tots.

RED OVEN PIZZA BAKERY Ω

Type: Quick Service

Description: Pizza table service

Open: Lunch and Dinner

Price: $$

Review: If you're craving pizza, this is the best spot in the Universal Orlando resort. The slices look like they came right out of a New York pizza spot with creamy melted mozzarella and large pepperonis. The fun of Red Oven is watching the chefs toss the dough to make the pizzas. A pie runs about $13 and is big enough for one person. They also have smaller pizzas for kids.

Menu Items: Pizza, salad, beer, wine, soda

Kids: chicken fingers, mini burgers, pasta, chicken with rice, waffle

Recommendation: Prosciutto and Arugula Pizza

TOOTHSOME CHOCOLATE EMPORIUM

Type: Table service and dessert bar

Description: Sweets and dishes in a steampunk theme

Open: Lunch and Dinner (also serves Brunch all day)

Price: $$-$$$

Review: The theme is like Charlie and the Chocolate Factory meets 19th century steampunk. The decor is stunning and the food looks mouthwatering. For mechanical gears to wild costumes, there's plenty to see around the room while you wait for a seat. We love looking at the array of desserts like fancy chocolates. Once seated, you'll have to resist ordering a little bit of everything. Since Toothsome's best designs are sweets, we recommend getting the brunch for lunch or dinner (they serve it all day).

Menu Items: Flatbreads, salads, soups, sandwiches, hamburgers, pasta, chicken, steak, crepes, quiche, waffles, French toast, milkshakes, desserts, beer, full bar, cocktails, wine, soda

Kids: chicken fingers, mini burgers, pasta, chicken with rice, waffle

Recommendation:

Appetizer: Philly Cheesesteak rolls

Entrees: Blackened Steak and Blue Flatbread – blue cheese, steak, caramelized onions, mushrooms, and spinach. Very flavorful!

Note: Toothsome also serves all-day brunch with sweet crepes and waffles that are worth ordering!

VIVO ITALIAN KITCHEN Ω

Type: Table Service

Price: $$-$$$

Description: Trendy Italian table service

Open: Lunch and Dinner

Review: There are two great Italian choices in the resort: Mama Della's Ristorante in the Portofino Bay Hotel and Vivo Italian Kitchen in CityWalk. While Mama Della's gives a more authentic Italian vibe, Vivo brings the trendy atmosphere. Try anything from pizza to pasta and Caesar salad to swordfish.

Menu Items: Pizza, pasta, salad, bolognese, lasagna, fish, chicken, lamb, wine, beer, specialty drinks, soda

Kids: spaghetti and meatball, pizza, chicken breast, shrimp skewer, meatball sandwiches

Recommendation: the bolognese

MORE EATS

Auntie Anne's Pretzels ($) – Delicious soft pretzels. We recommend the Cinnamon Sugar Nuggets, pretzel bits covered in cinnamon and sugar

Bread Box Handcrafted Sandwiches ($-$$) Ω – A corner store deli with handmade sandwiches. These are pretty good, especially the BLTA – Bacon, Arugula, Tomato, Balsamic mayonnaise, avocado sandwich

Cinnabon ($) – Delectable warm and frosted cinnamon rolls

Cold Stone ($) – Ice cream made to order

Dippin' Dot ($) – Hyper frozen ice cream beads

Fat Tuesday ($) – Alcoholic smoothie counter (for those 21 and older). Some of these can be extremely sweet, but we recommend the Peach bellini

Fusion Bistro Sushi and Sake Bar ($-$$) – Watch sushi chefs create rolls for you. Cowfish is still our favorite sushi spot at Universal, but if you're dining here, try the Shrimp tempura roll.

Hot Dog Hall of Fame ($-$$) Ω – Creative hot dogs inspired by the ball parks. Italian Sausage (with provolone, grilled onions, and peppers) is tasty!

Menchie's Frozen Yogurt ($) – self-serve froyo

Moe's Southwest Grill ($-$$) – Tex Mex Counter Service. Try the Homewrecker Burrito – a huge burrito stuffed with rice, beans, cheese, pico de gallo, guacamole, and sour cream. We recommend it with chicken or steak.

Panda Express ($-$$) – Quick to order Chinese food. Their glazed orange chicken is one of the best in the world.

Starbucks ($) – America's top choice for coffee

Whopper Bar by Burger King ($-$$) – Burger King's more upscale flame-broiled burgers. Try the Bourbon Burger, a beef patty with cheddar, bourbon sauce, and onion rings

Voodoo Doughnut ($) ♥ – Grab a specialty donut inspired by Universal films. These deserts are delicious and Voodoo is open late, until midnight on weekdays and 1AM on the weekends.

HOTEL DINING

HARD ROCK HOTEL

BEACHCLUB
Description: Poolside bar and grill
Type: Table service and bar
Open: Lunch and Dinner
Price: $$
Review: The Beachclub is an excellent choice for casual dining. No shirt? No problem! The waiters and bartenders serve those dressed or in their swimsuits. Oh, and the drinks are very delicious!
Menu Items: nachos, wings, quesadilla, loaded fries, ahi tuna, cheese sticks, pizza, egg roll, chips and salsa, edamame, tacos, burgers, wraps, hot dogs, smoothies, cocktails, and soda

For Kids: pizza, grilled cheese, mini burger, mac n cheese

Adult Beverages: mojitos, spiked lemonade, various cocktails, spiked slushies, margaritas, beer, wines, bloody Mary

Recommendations: Loaded Nachos – tortilla chips, cheese, lettuce, tomato, sour cream, guacamole, pico de gallo, and optional chicken or beef.

THE KITCHEN

Description: New American cuisine with 50's high-end rock diner feel

Type: Table service

Open: Breakfast, Lunch, Dinner

Price: $$ – $$$

Review: Delicious American food with friendly waiters and a restaurant that's fun to experience. The music is great and the prices aren't too shabby. For breakfast, they offer a buffet or a la carte. Kids under 3 eat at the buffet for free with a paying adult. The lunch and dinners menus are very similar in portion and price. If you're looking for something different, try the gator tail—it's surprisingly flavorful!

Menu Items:

Breakfast: omelet station, griddle station, muffins, pastries, breakfast pizza, yogurt, cottage cheese, scrambled eggs, biscuits and gravy, waffles, pancakes, bacon, sausage, sticky buns, corned beef hash, fruit, cereal, grits, oatmeal

Lunch and Dinner: Flatbreads, pasta, spinach and artichoke dip, soup, calamari, gator tail, quesadilla, burger, chicken and waffle, tacos, chicken potpie, short ribs, steak, shrimp, ahi tuna, cocktails, soda

For Kids: grilled cheese, hot dog, fries, turkey sandwich, peanut butter and jelly sandwich, burger, pizza, chicken tenders

Recommendation: The Kitchen Burger, an Angus beef, bacon, cheddar, onion rings, lettuce, tomato, and chipotle aioli. It's big and good!

· Magic Tip ·

Feeling extra hungry? Try the Kitchen Sink Challenge. If you can eat the Kitchen Burger, 1 pound of fries, a fried pickle, and a 7-layer kitchen sink cake in under 30 minutes, your meal is free.

PALM RESTAURANT ♥

Description: American steakhouse

Type: Table service
Open: Dinner
Price: $$ – $$$

Review: If you're looking for a bit more of an upscale affair, put Palm Steakhouse on your list. Serving up turf and surf, you can enjoy everything from mouthwatering steak to succulent lobsters. The food and the staff here are fantastic and steak lovers will leave very satisfied. The Palm also has a wide variety of wines and a full bar. We wish the décor was a little bit more fun, but the classic 1920's atmosphere is fun enough with your savory meal.

Menu Items: steak, lobster, salad, Italian, seafood, vegetables, and dessert. Also a variety of wines, cocktails, and soda.

For Kids: mozzarella sticks, steak, fries, mac n cheese, cheeseburger, grilled cheese sandwich, pasta, chicken strips

Recommendations: Filet Mignon, House Specialty Nova Scotia Lobster, or both with the Surf and Turf

Note: *Palm asks that guests come in resort or business casual wear, as sleeveless shirts and beachwear are not permitted.*

MORE EATS

Room Service
Staying in? Why not enjoy American favorites delivered right to your room? Hard Rock's room service is great, but can get a little slow late at night. If you're immediately hungry, just understand that you may have to wait up to an hour before you get your order.

PORTOFINO BAY

BICE RISTORANTE
Description: Traditional Italian
Type: Upscale table service
Open: Dinner
Price: $$$
Review: A perfect intimate scene that transports you to Italy. Friendly staff serve delicious Italian food in an authentic way with

several courses. Though the menu is similar to Mama Della's, the food has a different flare of seasonings. Come in cocktail or business casual attire. We prefer Mama Della's because the prices are better than Bice and we think the food is tastier. However, if you're looking for an upscale dining experience, Bice won't disappoint. Don't worry if you can't pronounce the words, the waiters are used to it and happy that you tried you best!

Menu Items: Pasta, soup, antipasta, insalate, veal, steak, Italian desserts, wine, soda

Recommendation: Anitpasto all'Italiana con Salumi, Ravioli di Manzo all Massaia, Petto Di Pollo ripieno di Fontina, Crème Cotta alla Vaniglia – vanilla crème brule

MAMA DELLA'S RISTORANTE ♥

Description: Homestyle Italian Restaurant
Type: Table service
Open: Dinner
Price: $$$
Review: One of the best restaurants on the resort! We love Mama Della's for its tasty Italian cuisine, charming performers, and overall aesthetics. Perfect for special occasions, let the singers serenade you in the intimate venue—a few dollars in cash tips are recommended. The menu keeps pretty close to homestyle American Italian meals, so come hungry!

Menu Items: Pasta, soup, calamari, scampi, caprese, antipasto, ravioli, cabonara, gnocchi, eggplant parmesan, lasagna, vegetarian, wine, soda

For Kids: macaroni and cheese, fettuccine alfredo, spaghetti and meatballs, pizza, peanut butter and jelly sandwich, buttered noodles and ham, lasagna, chicken fingers

Recommendations: Calamari fritti, Gnocchi al Pomodoro or Lasagna ♥, Tiramisu

TRATTORIA DEL PORTO

Description: Family Italian and American Breakfast
Type: American and Italian Casual dining
Open: Breakfast, Lunch and Dinner
Price: $$
Review: One of the better restaurants for the whole family. Dine on Italian favorites and meet some characters like the Minions from *Despicable Me*. The environment is much more casual than the

other Portofino Bay restaurants, so everyone can feel relaxed as they enjoy some good food.

Menu Items: Breakfast: baked goods, eggs, bacon, hash browns, pancakes, waffles, French toast, eggs benedict, breakfast wraps, steak and eggs, custom omelets, smoothies, fruit, oatmeal, cereal, banana split, juice

Lunch: soup, salad, flatbread, sandwiches, burgers, pasta, dessert, wine, beer, soda

Dinner: soup, salad, flatbread, sandwiches, burgers, pasta, steak, swordfish, shrimp and grits, salmon, dessert, wine, beer, soda

Kids: quesadilla, hot dog, French fries, pizza, chicken fingers, peanut butter and jelly, cheeseburger, steak, fettuccini alfredo, punch

Recommendations:
Breakfast: Eggs Benedicto – eggs, prosciutto, arugula, and hollandaise on ciabatta bread
Lunch: Citrus Marinated Chicken Sandwich – lettuce, tomatoes, pepper jack cheese, aioli
Dinner: Grilled Chicken Sandwich – lettuce, tomatoes, cheddar, bacon, aioli

Note: *For character dining, visit Friday nights from 6:30PM – 9:30PM.*

MORE EATS

Room Service – Open 24 hours a day, 7 days a week with American favorites from burgers to pizza and kids' items, too.

Sal's Market Deli – Pizzas and Italian made to order. Try the prosciutto or Margherita pizza. The large is perfect for sharing! Fast and inexpensive compared to the table service places.

Splendido Bar and Grill – A poolside bar and grill with a lax environment. Stroll in for a drink, burger, or salad.

Gelateria – Sample from several types of gelato. Pick your favorite and stroll the water way.

Starbucks – America's #1 coffee chain is open daily from 6AM – 8PM

ROYAL PACIFIC

JAKE'S AMERICAN BAR

Description: American Favorites and full bar
Type: Casual table service
Open: Lunch and Dinner
Price: $$

Menu Items: cheese board, calamari, hot wings, cheese fries, salad, soup, burgers, sandwiches, chicken, fish and chips, steak, pasta, short ribs, flatbread, pizza, full bar, soda, wine, cocktails
Kids: burger, sandwich, quesadilla, fries, chicken tenders
Late Night: beef and cheese fries, bacon burger, Caesar salad, hot wings, pizzas

Review: Jake's feels like a place someone who owns a propeller plane or a boat might like to hang out after work. It's a relaxed island vibe centered around a full bar with a lot of choices. The food isn't as good as the high price suggests. Expect to pay $15-$30 for an entrée, but these *are* amusement park prices. Jake's wins points for being open late with a late-night menu that's not too pricey (open until 1:30am).

Recommendation: B-1 Bomber Burger (standard burger with bacon)

ORCHID COURT LOUNGE & SUSHI BAR

Description: Sushi Bar
Type: Japanese
Open: Lunch and Dinner
Price: $$

Review: A simple sushi bar inside of the hotel. Focuses mostly around the drinks, but you can get rolls ordered at a decent price. The rolls are pretty tasty!

BULA BAR AND GRILL

Description: Our door bar with food
Type: American and Polynesian
Open: Lunch and Dinner
Price: $$

Review: A simple outdoor bar near the pool. Come dressed in your casual or pool clothing and order a drink or something to eat.

The food is quite good though we recommend sticking with standards like sliders, quesadilla, or a burger for the better flavors.

MORE EATS

Room Service – Open 24 hours a day, 7 days a week with American favorites from burgers to pizza and kids' items, too.

SAPPHIRE FALLS

AMATISTA COOKHOUSE
Description: Caribbean and American
Type: Table service
Open: Breakfast, Lunch, and Dinner
Price: $$-$$$
Review: With a blend of ocean and land dishes, Amatista Cookhouse aims at the trendy, almost posh vibe you'd find in Miami or Los Angeles. Yet, the décor is simple, so dining hear doesn't feel as exclusive as big city restaurants. The food is decent, but nothing too special. You'll get the typical food found around Universal Orlando, so you may want to head to CityWalk for even the pool bar, Drhum Club Kantine that has similar and less expensive food. Still, there are some great dishes here. We recommend Amatista for breakfast, too.
Menu Items:
Breakfast: eggs, bacon, omelet, fruit, granola, pancakes, waffles, French toast, smoked salmon, cereal, muffin, juice, tea, coffee, soda
Lunch and Dinner: wings, empanadas, chowder, salad, fries, pizza, flatbread, pork chop, steak, burger, sandwiches
Recommendation:
Breakfast: Caribbean French toast
Lunch or Dinner: Amatista Caribbean Burger

DRHUM CLUB KANTINE
Price: $$
Description: Snacks and Drinks
Type: Casual table service

Open: Lunch and Dinner
Review: Head outside and dine on tasty bar snacks and meals.
Menu Items:
Lunch and Dinner: Nachos, wings, empanadas, salad, fish, burgers, sandwiches, ice cream, margaritas, full bar
Kids: chicken fingers, grilled cheese, burger, hot dog, grilled chicken
Recommendation: Nachos or Fish Taco

MORE EATS

New Dutch Trading Co. – Grab ice cream, smoothies, shakes, and even sandwiches, cake and donuts from this stack stop.

Strong Water Tavern – A collection of vintage rums to dazzle adult senses. You can also try several tapas from around the world to pair with your choice of drink. As the bartender what he recommends! There's always something new to try.

Room Service – Open 24 hours a day, 7 days a week with American favorites from burgers to pizza and kids' items, too.

CABANA BAY

GALAXY BOWL RESTAURANT
Description: American
Type: Quick Service
Open: Lunch and Dinner from 11am – 10pm
Review: Family friendly cuisine to match with your day or night of bowling. The food is pretty good and a great price. Most of the meals are under $10.
Price: $-$$
Menu Items: Burgers, wraps, sandwiches, wings, quesadillas, pizza, soda, mixed drinks, beer, wine
Kids: chicken fingers, grilled cheese, mac and cheese
What to Order: Galaxy Burger or Bacon Cheese Burger

THE HIDEAWAY BAR AND GRILLE
Price: $$
Description: Snacks and Drinks
Type: Poolside
Open: Lunch and Dinner
Review: Hang by the pool and dine on American favorites
Menu Items: Hot dogs, salads, fries, sandwiches, wraps, burgers, soda, juice, cocktails, beer
Kids: chicken fingers, grilled cheese, burger, fish sticks, peanut butter and jelly sandwich
Recommendation: Honolulu Hot Dog or Turkey Club Wrap

MORE EATS

Starbucks – Coffee, pastries, and breakfast items

Atomic Tonic – An outdoor bar with specialty drinks and sandwiches, wraps, salads, and skewers. Try the delicious Cabana Bay Colada!

Delizioso Pizza – Pick up or order a pizza pie delivered to your room. Pizzas are about 10" and deliver from 10am – Midnight, and until 1am on Friday and Saturday nights. Call (407) 503-4300 for delivery.

Room Service – Open 24 hours a day, 7 days a week with American favorites from burgers to pizza and kids' items, too.

AVENTURA

BAR 17 BISTRO
Description: Rooftop dining and bar
Type: Table Service
Open: Snacks and Dinner from 5pm - 10pm, Drinks from 4pm - 2am (though it may close early on less popular nights).
Review: Adult-oriented dining and full bar
Price: $$
Menu Items: bao buns, beef sliders, chicken, rice and noodles, grilled octopus, meat and cheese board, salads, full bar
What to Order: Braise Pork Belly bao bun, wagyu beef sliders, summer beet & glazed fig salad

URBAN PANTRY
Price: $$
Description: American, Asian, and European-inspired dining
Type: Quick Service
Open: Breakfast, Lunch, and Dinner (7am - 11pm on most nights)
Review: Urban Pantry offers a wider variety of bites not usually offered in the Universal Orlando Resort. There's something for everyone here.
Menu Items:
Breakfast: omelets, breakfast sandwiches, pastries, continental breakfast items, flatbreads, full bar
Lunch & Dinner: build-your-own wok, tuna poke, sushi, pizza, burgers, paella, chicken, carving station, full bar
Kids: chicken fingers, grilled cheese, burger, fish sticks, peanut butter and jelly sandwich
Recommendation: Build-your-own wok or a burger

MORE EATS

Starbucks – Coffee, pastries, and breakfast items

Bar Sol – a poolside bar

barVentura – a lobby lounge bar

Room Service – Open 24 hours a day, 7 days a week with American favorites from burgers to pizza and kids' items, too. You can order from the tablet in your room!

CHAPTER ELEVEN

HALLOWEEN HORROR NIGHTS

INTRODUCTION

If Halloween is one of your favorite holidays, it might be time to book a trip to Universal Studios Orlando in autumn! Halloween Horror Nights is an epic, park-wide scare zone with haunted mazes, creepy treats, spooky stage shows—and so much more! Mostly popular with adults, the park transforms at sundown into a terrifying and ghastly world! You'll see your favorite horror movies and scary TV series come to life in this unique experience.

Halloween Horror Nights (HHN) is a separate ticketed nighttime event that takes place in just one of the parks (usually Universal Studios, but sometimes Islands of Adventure). Most of the rides are open with the addition of haunted mazes. Starting at the entrance, creepy demons and "serial killers" roam foggy streets. Each year holds a new set of terrifying surprises.

WHEN IS HHN?

The event takes place from mid-September through the first week of November. Tickets sell out faster closer to Halloween.

WHAT ARE THE SCARE ZONES AND MAZES?

Scare Zones and Mazes are frightening areas where horror franchises come to life. You might be chased by a chainsaw-wielding Jason or escape the wrath of killers from *The Purge* series. *American Horror Story*, *Nightmare on Elm Street*, *The Walking Dead*, *The Shining*, and *Saw* have all made appearances at HHN. Universal usually begins announcing maze and scare zone themes in the summer before the event.

SHOULD I BRING MY CHILD?

Probably not. Even if your kid can handle watching a horror movie, they might feel way too scared when a gang of nightmarish creatures chases them down the street. We sometimes do see kids at HHN, and we've also seen many of them crying their eyes out. The general consensus is that the event is for teens and older. So, wait until your child turns 13 and you can reexamine if they are ready.

PURCHASING DISCOUNTED TICKETS

Buy early! Universal announces Halloween Horror Nights usually six months before the event. Tickets will be cheaper as you buy them earlier with prices hiking in the late summer—and even higher after that. Also, popular dates sell out quickly (like weekends and Halloween night). The least-expensive tickets are in September through the first week of October. Weekdays are also the cheaper (though HHN isn't open on every weeknight). If you are planning on visiting more than one night, season passes are also available.

Universal will often hold a promotion with Coca-Cola or other popular brand for discounted tickets on select dates. These discounts are usually listed before purchasing tickets: www.HalloweenHorrorNights.com.

Note: *We have seen many people purchase the wrong Halloween Horror Night tickets. When visiting the website, make sure that you are purchasing tickets for Orlando and not Hollywood.*

PREPARING FOR LONG LINES

The event becomes more crowded the closer to Halloween. Many times, weekday tickets (excluding Friday) don't sell out in the weeks before Halloween. Three to five hour long wait times have been reported for some of the popular mazes on crowded nights. If you're planning on a crowded night, get there at the start of the event to experience the mazes before the bulk of the crowd. You can also purchase an Express Pass (usually $85-$100 extra) to skip the lines and complete them all.

EXPRESS PASS

You likely won't get to experience every maze in a single night without Express Pass. Even if you go when the sun is still out at the start of the event, it's very difficult to get through the bulk of the mazes. Every year, there are very popular mazes that have the longest lines. We update the top choices in our free e-mail newsletter (sign up at: **www.magicguidebooks.com/list**). Keep in mind, the daytime Express Pass will not work for HHN and hotel guest Express Passes also do not work for this event.

· **Magic Tip** ·

Universal sells Express Passes that work after 10PM for about half of the normal cost. To save money and time, we recommend buying one of these at the start of your night as they tend to sell out before 10PM. Look for an Express Pass distribution kiosk.

CHAPTER TWELVE

BEST-OF LISTS

INTRODUCTION

Though we do our best to condense the information in this book, we recognize that it can still feel fairly stuffed. As you're planning your trip, you may feel that there are far too many options to choose from. To help sort these options, we've compiled valuable lists with our most recommended experiences. In this chapter, we highlight the best that the Universal Orlando Resort has to offer to make the most of your vacation.

Note: *We determined these lists by fun, uniqueness, and consistency of the experience. The food was determined by flavor, quality, and uniqueness.*

BEST-OF LISTS

BEST RIDES AND ATTRACTIONS
1. Harry Potter and the Forbidden Journey (Islands of Adventure)
2. Revenge of the Mummy (Universal Studios)
3. The Incredible Hulk Coaster (Islands of Adventure)
4. Jurassic Park River Adventure (Islands of Adventure)
5. Harry Potter and the Escape from Gringotts (Universal Studios)
6. Dudley Do-Right's Ripsaw Falls (Islands of Adventure)
7. Hollywood Rip Ride Rockit (Universal Studios)

BEST RESTAURANTS
1. The Three Broomsticks (Islands of Adventure, Hogsmeade)
2. Mama Della's Ristorante (Loew's Portofino Hotel)
3. The Leaky Cauldron (Universal Studios, Diagon Alley)
4. The Cowfish (CityWalk)
5. Bubba Gump Shrimp Co. (CityWalk)
6. Thunder Falls Terrace (Islands of Adventure, Jurassic Park)
7. The Kitchen (Hard Rock Hotel)

HONORABLE MENTIONS
- Confisco Grille (Islands of Adventure, Port of Entry)
- Circus McGurkus Café Stoo-pendous (Islands of Adventure, Seuss Landing)

BEST TREATS AND SNACKS
1. Butterbeer (Both Parks, Butterbeer station at Diagon Alley and Hogsmeade Village)
2. Big Pink (Universal Studios, Lard Lad's in Springfield)
3. Butterbeer Potted Cream (Both Parks, Leaky Cauldron in Diagon Alley and Three Broomsticks in Hogsmeade Village)
4. Flaming Moe [non-alcoholic] (Universal Studios, Flaming Moe's in Springfield)
5. Pumpkin Juice (Both Parks, Butterbeer station at Diagon Alley and Hogsmeade Village)
6. Any Dessert at Toothsome! (CityWalk, Toothsome Chocolate Emporium)
7. Lava Flow [alcoholic and non-alcoholic] (City Walk, Bubba Gump's Shrimp Co.)

CHAPTER THIRTEEN

PRE-PLANNED
RIDE AND ATTRACTION
GUIDES

INTRODUCTION

Many who visit Universal Orlando are worried about experiencing everything they want during their stay. With so many choices, it might be impossible to get everything done in one day without a plan. However, with our pre-made ride and attraction lists, you can enjoy the very best that Universal has to offer. These are *proven* to work using multiple tests over several visits. Thus, we recommend following one of our pre-made touring plans in order accomplish the best on a busy day— even if you don't purchase Express Pass!

Before you get started in the Parks, make sure you complete these steps:

1. Choose one of our pre-made ride and attraction lists to follow.
2. Get to the Park before it opens.
3. Grab a map at the entrance to help guide you around.
4. Prepare to take a break when you need to in between rides.
5. Don't rush. Keep calm, enjoy the sights, and take in the fun!

UNIVERSAL STUDIOS FLORIDA

1. **Harry Potter and the Escape from Gringotts** (Diagon Alley)
2. **Ollivanders** (Diagon Alley)
3. **Explore Diagon Alley**
4. **Fast & Furious – Supercharged** (San Francisco)
5. **Hollywood Rip Ride Rockit** (New York)
6. **Revenge of the Mummy** (New York)
7. **Race Through New York Starring Jimmy Fallon** (New York)
8. **Despicable Me Minion Mayhem** (Production Central)
9. **Shrek 4-D (Production Central)**
10. **E. T. Adventure** (Woody Woodpecker's Kid Zone)
11. **MEN IN BLACK Alien Attack** (World's Fair)
12. **The Simpsons Ride** (Springfield)
13. **TRANSFORMERS: The Ride-3D** (New York)
14. **Universal Orlando's Cinematic Celebration** (nighttime show)

Dining Recommendation:
Leaky Cauldron (Diagon Alley)

ISLANDS OF ADVENTURE

1. **Harry Potter and the Forbidden Journey** (Hogsmeade Village)
2. **Flight of the Hippogriff** (Hogsmeade Village)
3. **Ollivanders** (Hogsmeade Village)
4. **Explore Hogsmeade Village**
5. **Raptor Encounter** (Jurassic Park)
6. **Jurassic Park River Adventure** (Jurassic Park)
7. **Dudley Do-Right's Ripsaw Falls** (Toon Lagoon)
8. **Popeye & Bluto's Bilge-Rat Barges** (Toon Lagoon)
9. **Doctor Doom's Fearfall** (Marvel Super Hero Island)
10. **The Amazing Adventures of Spider-Man** (Marvel Super Hero Island)
11. **The Incredible Hulk Coaster** (Marvel Super Hero Island)
12. **The Cat in the Hat** (Marvel Super Hero Island)
13. **Poseidon's Fury** (The Lost Continent)
14. **The Nighttime Lights at Hogwarts Castle** (Hogsmeade Village)

Dining Recommendation:
Three Broomsticks (Hogsmeade Village)

Note: *When the new Harry Potter roller coaster opens (Fall 2019), we recommend experiencing that attraction first in your day at Islands of Adventure.*

UNIVERSAL ORLANDO
BOTH PARKS IN ONE DAY

* = If you did not purchase Express Pass, you may want to skip these rides and experience the others first.

Ω = Better for Young Kids than Teens and Adults

† = Extreme Coaster or Attraction

UNIVERSAL STUDIOS FLORIDA
1. **Harry Potter and the Escape from Gringotts** (Diagon Alley)
2. **Ollivanders** (Diagon Alley)
3. **Explore Diagon Alley** (limit to 25 minutes)
4. **Hogwarts Express** (to Universal Islands of Adventure)

UNIVERSAL ISLANDS OF ADVENTURE
1. **Harry Potter and the Forbidden Journey** (Hogsmeade Village)
2. **Flight of the Hippogriff** (Hogsmeade Village)
3. **Explore Hogsmeade Village** (limit to 25 minutes)
4. **Jurassic Park River Adventure** (Jurassic Park)
5. **Dudley Do-Right's Ripsaw Falls** (Toon Lagoon)
6. **Popeye & Bluto's Bilge-Rat Barges** (Toon Lagoon)*
7. **Doctor Doom's Fearfall** (Marvel Super Hero Island) †
8. **The Amazing Adventures of Spider-Man** (Marvel Super Hero Island)
9. **Incredible Hulk Coaster** (Marvel Super Hero Island) †
10. **The Cat in the Hat** (Marvel Super Hero Island) Ω
11. **Hogwarts Express** (to Universal Studios Florida)

UNIVERSAL STUDIOS FLORIDA
12. **Fast & Furious – Supercharged** (San Francisco)*
13. **Hollywood Rip Ride Rockit** (New York) †
14. **Revenge of the Mummy** (New York)
15. **Race Through New York Starring Jimmy Fallon** (New York)*
16. **Despicable Me Minion Mayhem** (Production Central) Ω
17. **Shrek 4-D (Production Central)** * Ω

18. **E. T. Adventure** (Woody Woodpecker's Kid Zone) Ω
19. **MEN IN BLACK Alien Attack** (World's Fair)
20. **The Simpsons Ride** (Springfield)
21. **TRANSFORMERS: The Ride-3D** (New York)
22. **Universal Orlando's Cinematic Celebration** (nighttime show)

Note: *When the new Harry Potter roller coaster opens (Fall 2019), we recommend experiencing that attraction when you first visit Hogsmeade Village.*

CUSTOM RIDE LIST

Park(s): _____

Names: _____   _____

_____   _____

_____   _____

1. _____
2. _____
3. _____
4. _____
5. _____
6. _____
7. _____
8. _____
9. _____
10. _____
11. _____
12. _____
13. _____
14. _____
15. _____
16. _____
17. _____
18. _____
19. _____
20. _____
21. _____
22. _____
23. _____
24. _____
25. _____

CUSTOM RIDE LIST

Park(s): _____

Names: _____   _____
        _____   _____
        _____   _____

1. _____
2. _____
3. _____
4. _____
5. _____
6. _____
7. _____
8. _____
9. _____
10. _____
11. _____
12. _____
13. _____
14. _____
15. _____
16. _____
17. _____
18. _____
19. _____
20. _____
21. _____
22. _____
23. _____
24. _____
25. _____

CUSTOM RIDE LIST

Park(s): _____

Names: _____   _____

_____   _____

_____   _____

1. _____
2. _____
3. _____
4. _____
5. _____
6. _____
7. _____
8. _____
9. _____
10. _____
11. _____
12. _____
13. _____
14. _____
15. _____
16. _____
17. _____
18. _____
19. _____
20. _____
21. _____
22. _____
23. _____
24. _____
25. _____

CUSTOM RIDE LIST

Park(s): _____

Names: _____   _____
         _____   _____
         _____   _____

1. _____
2. _____
3. _____
4. _____
5. _____
6. _____
7. _____
8. _____
9. _____
10. _____
11. _____
12. _____
13. _____
14. _____
15. _____
16. _____
17. _____
18. _____
19. _____
20. _____
21. _____
22. _____
23. _____
24. _____
25. _____

VACATION CHECKLIST

- ❑ Park Tickets
- ❑ Ride List
- ❑ ID
- ❑ Credit Card / Cash
- ❑ Hotel Address
- ❑ Phone (and charging cable)
- ❑ Sunscreen
- ❑ Toiletries: toothbrush, toothpaste, etc.
- ❑ Swimsuit
- ❑ Jacket
- ❑ Comfortable Shoes
- ❑ Plastic bag for cellphone (water rides)
- ❑ Snacks
- ❑ Water bottles (if you aren't flying)
- ❑ Backpack or bag
- ❑ Restaurant Reservations
- ❑ Universal Orlando 2019 by Magic Guidebooks
- ❑ _____
- ❑ _____
- ❑ _____
- ❑ _____
- ❑ _____
- ❑ _____
- ❑ _____
- ❑ _____
- ❑ _____
- ❑ _____

CONCLUSION
AND THE FUTURE OF THE
UNIVERSAL ORLANDO RESORT

The Universal Orlando Resort is always changing and so will this guide throughout the years. This is our second version in the series and we want to thank you for supporting us! We sincerely hope that this book is a valuable resource for you. As noted at the beginning, we are theme park fans and we've created this guide from our firsthand knowledge and research.

Universal has promised to keep creating for years to come. Recently, they've acquired hundreds of acres of land, which could signal a third park. So far, Universal hasn't confirmed this, but guest surveys reveal that a theme park called "Fantastic Worlds" might be on the way! We would expect many more franchises such *Fantastic Beasts and Where to Find Them* and *How to Train Your Dragon*.

Universal also recently closed the unpopular stunt show, The Many Voyages of Sinbad, which happens to be located next to Hogsmeade Village. Could this mean an expansion of the Harry Potter Universe? We're heard rumors of a Quidditch-based attraction and Universal has even patented several show-style conccpts that could host such an awesome attraction.

With the Walt Disney World Resort's 50th anniversary coming in 2021, Universal will aim to give traveling guests a reason to visit its resort. Beginning back in 2017, Universal had also promised to open a new hotel every year for the next ten years. So far, they've kept this promise!

To conclude, we'd like to invite you to stay connected with us. Our website, **magicguidebooks.com**, is packed with new information and details about Universal and Disney theme parks. Small parts of this book may need updating due to Universal's constant changes, however, we keep you up to speed in our newsletter to improve your vacation experience.

Happy and safe travels!
Magic Guidebooks

INDEX

A

airline, 34, 41-43
alcoholic beverages, 14, 32, 124, 135, 139, 156
Amazing Adventures of Spider-Man, The, 53, 67-68
AMC Universal Cineplex 20, 114
American Express, 17, 26, 37, 119
American Express Lounge, 26, 37
Animal Actors on Location, 62
annual pass, 35
app, 15
author, information, 5
Aventura Hotel, 27-28, 105-106, 149

B

Barney the Purple Dinosaur, 50, 62
best days to visit, 21-22
Blue Man Group, 113
Blue the Velociraptor, 77
Blues Brothers Show, The, 55
boats (see ferries)
bracelets (see TapuTapu)
buffets, 27-29, 99, 102, 141
bus, 45-46
business center, 92, 95, 99, 109
Butterbeer, 12, 14, 28, 75, 119, 122, 125, 129, 130-131, 156

C

Cabana Bay, 27-29, 103-105, 147-148
cabs (see taxi)
Camp Jurassic, 66, 77
car, driving by, 44
car rental, 44
Caro-Seuss-El, 69
cash, 118, 120
castle (see Hogwarts Castle)
Cat in the Hat, The, 66, 69
character dining, 27-29, 120-121, 126, 144
Christmas, 22. 28-29
CityWalk (see Universal CityWalk)
club level, 91, 94-95, 98

G

H

I

J

K

DINING

We did not index most restaurants as they are available in alphabetical order by resort area in the Dining Guide (Chapter 15).

GET UPDATES!
Universal Orlando 2019

Sign up for our FREE e-mail list!

www.magicguidebooks.com/signup
(We will never spam your information)

Wishing you a magical vacation!
Magic Guidebooks

Made in the USA
Lexington, KY
13 February 2019